Service-Learning
Course Design for
Community Colleges

Service-Learning Course Design for Community Colleges

By Marina Baratian
Donna Killian Duffy
Robert Franco
Amy Hendricks
and Tanya Renner

with a foreword by
Kay McClenney

Campus Compact

Campus Compact

Brown University
Box 1975
Providence, RI 02912

phone: 401-867-3950
email: campus@compact.org
website: www.compact.org

About Campus Compact

Campus Compact is a national coalition of more than 1,000 college and university presidents—representing some 6 million students—who are committed to fulfilling the civic purposes of higher education. As the only national association dedicated solely to this mission, Campus Compact is a leader in building civic engagement into campus and academic life. Through our national office and network of 32 state offices, members receive the training, resources, and advocacy they need to build strong surrounding communities and teach students the skills and values of democracy.

Campus Compact's membership includes public, private, two- and four-year institutions across the spectrum of higher education. These institutions put into practice the ideal of civic engagement by sharing knowledge and resources with their communities, creating local development initiatives, and supporting service and service-learning efforts in areas such as literacy, health care, hunger, homelessness, and the environment.

Campus Compact comprises a national office based in Providence, RI, and state offices in CA, CO, CT, FL, HI, IA, IL, IN, KS, KY, LA, MA, ME, MI, MN, MO, MT, NC, NH, NY, OH, OK, OR, PA, RI, SC, TX, UT, VT, WA, WI, and WV. For contact and other information, see www.compact.org.

This material is based on work supported by the Corporation for National and Community Service under Learn and Serve Grant No. 00LHERI18800. Opinions or points of view expressed in this document are those of the authors and do not necessarily reflect the official position of the Corporation or the Learn and Serve America Program.

Cover and book design: Bonnie Grassie-Hughes

ISBN: 978-0-9729394-8-5

Table of Contents

List of Appendices

Foreword

On the Purposeful Engagement of Community College Students

An unequivocal finding of the research on undergraduate learning and success is that *student engagement matters*. That is, the more engaged students are—the more involved and connected they are with one another, with faculty and student affairs professionals, and with the subject matter of their studies—the more likely they are to persist in college and to learn at higher levels. And if student engagement matters across all sectors of higher education, it's easy to make the case that it may matter most for community college students.

Community colleges, we all know, are diverse institutions that serve remarkably diverse student populations. These students typically contend with competing priorities—juggling jobs, family responsibilities, financial struggles, and community commitments along with their academic endeavors. Given that reality, finding ways to engage community college students effectively is not easy; it's just essential. And it does not happen by accident; rather, it generally has to happen by design.

The Community College Survey of Student Engagement (CCSSE) was established in 2001 and is based on research about effective educational practice. Over the course of five national surveys, CCSSE now has polled almost 700,000 students from 550 different community colleges in 48 states. One of the unique contributions of the initiative has been to provide community colleges with national benchmarks of effective educational practice, enabling institutions to assess how they are doing, to benchmark their performance against groups of similar colleges, and to target improvements in programs and services for students. At its heart, CCSSE is not merely a survey; it's a change strategy.

The benchmarks, comprising related items on the survey, are: 1) active and collaborative learning; 2) student effort; 3) academic challenge; 4) student-faculty interaction; and 5) support for learners. Once colleges see their results on these benchmarks, the pivotal question, of course, is, "Now what?" Sometimes the appropriate response is to focus on the "low-hanging fruit"—the small changes that can be implemented immediately. Increasingly, though, community college leaders—including those among the faculty and staff—are realizing that we have large issues to address if we're serious about improving student persistence and learning.

These large issues demand large responses. By this I mean not a boutique program, not innovation on the margins, but the intentional redesign of students' educational experiences so they *cannot escape* engagement because it is so ingrained in college processes and programs.

An optimal solution to this challenge of intentional design is to incorporate service-learning across the community college curriculum. As illustrated throughout this book, service-learning, properly conceived and executed, powerfully reflects those key elements of the student experience that we know are important to learning and success: collaboration with other students and with community partners; active involvement in planning, participating in, and reflecting upon the service experience; focused interaction with faculty, peers, and others; and rigorous reflection and discussion that links acts of service with acts of substantive learning.

Beyond the benefits of that purposeful design of community college courses, though, is the powerful sense of *purposefulness* that service-learning brings to the educational experience. How often do we hear from these adult learners, these first-generation college-goers, these students so often alienated through their previous educational experiences, that they long for connections between what we ask them to learn and what is going on in their "real" lives? And what better way is there to help them than to create the conditions within which they may carve those connections for themselves, building purpose into both their studies and their lives?

In the most recent survey of community college students, only 6% indicated that they had often or very often participated in a community-based project as part of a course.[1] Fourteen percent reported "sometimes" participating, but the remainder said they never do. As those numbers increase, the benefits to individual students and to their communities will multiply. And in this book we find the concrete strategies for moving forward with that important work.

Kay M. McClenney,
Director of the Community College Survey of Student Engagement,
part of the Community College Leadership Program at
The University of Texas at Austin

---

1. Community College Survey of Student Engagement (2006). "Act On Fact: Using Data to Improve Student Success." Austin, TX: Community College Survey of Student Engagement, The University of Texas at Austin. Available at http://www.ccsse.org/publications/CCSSENationalReport2006.pdf.

Introduction

Campus Compact, Service-Learning, and Community College Engagement

DONNA KILLIAN DUFFY

WHY IS THERE A NEED FOR A BOOK ON SERVICE-LEARNING course design specifically for community colleges? By incorporating community work into the curriculum, service-learning not only addresses community needs but also helps students acquire hands-on experience that enhances academic learning. In the community college setting, service-learning thus can provide a valuable link between students' academic and community lives. Other benefits of service-learning, from retention to workforce readiness, are also well suited to the community college experience. Although many resources are available to help campuses incorporate service-learning into the curriculum, including several seminal works from Campus Compact (see, for example, *Fundamentals of Service-Learning Course Construction*, Heffernan, 2001), few address the specific needs of community colleges.

The idea for this book grew out of Campus Compact's Indicators of Engagement Project, which documented and disseminated best practices of civic engagement at different institutional types, including community colleges. This multi-year project examined engagement "indicators" across five broad categories: institutional culture, faculty roles and rewards, mechanisms and resources, community-campus exchange, and curriculum and pedagogy. One of the resulting publications, *The Community's College: Indicators of Engagement at Two-Year Institutions* (Zlotkowski et al., 2004), provides models and best practices within each category of engagement, drawn from community colleges across the country. The current volume delves more deeply into "curriculum and pedagogy," focusing on the practical aspects of implementing curriculum changes to support engagement at community colleges.

Faculty at community colleges contribute to engagement strategies at many levels, but their main focus is on creating engagement and community with students in their classrooms. As Spitzberg and Thorndike (1992) have written, "the classroom is the most logical, most visible, most ubiquitous, and most neglected place for community on campus. It is a lost opportunity of the first order" (p.116).

Faculty members can use service-learning to enhance the classroom community as well as to support civic engagement in local communities, but they have many questions about how to design courses in order to maximize both learning and community. The goals of this volume are to assist faculty in answering their questions about service-learning course design and to guide them in using the curriculum to advance engagement on their campuses.

The Next Level of Excellence

In *Creating Significant Learning Experiences,* Dee Fink (2003, p. 174) notes:

> Teaching well, to use an old adage, is not a destination but a journey. Even though there will likely be very good experiences along the way, one has to always look at oneself and in essence say: "This was good but not as good as it could be. I need to keep on working at it, to find some way of taking it to the next level of excellence."

Faculty engaged in service-learning at community colleges are committed to creating significant learning experiences for their students. These professors often report exciting experiences on their learning journeys but also report having limited time for analyzing such experiences because of the demands of high course loads and diverse student needs. In this volume, several practitioners with wide experience have stepped back to reflect on their service-learning work and to offer strategies for moving to the next level of excellence.

As educators we are part of a larger system of higher education with a unique opportunity to fulfill the community college's role. A key aspect of this role is to create a "genuinely egalitarian system of education that fosters the development of a citizenry fully equal to the arduous task of democratic self-governance" (Brint & Karabel, 1989, p. 232); bear in mind that community colleges were initially referred to as America's "democracy colleges."

The opportunity to serve as a democracy college can be overlooked by faculty as daily pressures to organize classes and correct papers demand immediate attention. Yet this opportunity is critical. As Robert Franco suggests in Chapter 1, "community colleges can catalyze ideas, issues, practices, and policies so that a renewed civic energy results in stronger citizens and communities." How can we be more deliberate in constructing service-learning courses into attainment pathways both for baccalaureate success and for civic outcomes? One practical suggestion is to assess the learning outcomes of courses—and to examine these outcomes within the broader student experience. As Franco emphasizes, for service-learning attainment pathways to be successful, "faculty and community partners need to take collective responsibility for helping students learn collective responsibility." In the following chapters of the volume, each author shares an aspect of teaching practice that will help in moving students closer to the goal of learning collective responsibility.

In Chapter 2, Amy Hendricks provides a detailed guide to designing a course syllabus that includes a service-learning component, with concrete advice for those new to this process as well as strategies for experienced practitioners to take this work to new levels. Having a vision of our institutions as democracy colleges is uplifting, but it needs to be supported with concrete ideas for dealing with a classroom of diverse students who may vary widely in their passion for significant learning experiences. Often community issues that resonate with students' lives provide excellent ways to engage students in learning course concepts. But, as Hendricks states, the issues addressed by students' service must come from the community, not from students or faculty. Given this reality, how can faculty select community sites that will help students achieve their course objectives? What types of activities at the site will have the greatest impact on students' learning? This chapter reviews such questions and includes examples from a wide range of courses to provide answers.

The majority of community college students are juggling multiple responsibilities in their lives. This means that most classes at community colleges include service-learning as an option in the course, rather than as a requirement. However, as Marina Baratian demonstrates in Chapter 3, creating a course that requires service as the main focus can result in a customized experience unique to the personal needs and goals of students in the class. This chapter presents a continuum of choices for stand-alone courses, from a three-credit Community Involvement course to an Honors Community Involvement course to a Service-Learning Fourth-Credit Option. Baratian includes specific details about each of these alternatives so readers can easily employ the model or adjust it for different course needs. Faculty who have been using service-learning as a course option for some time may find that moving to a stand-alone model represents a way of taking their effective practice to Fink's "next level of excellence."

In Chapter 4, Tanya Renner focuses on the importance of assessing service-learning outcomes and notes that through such assessments, institutions may find that they are simultaneously assessing results related to efforts to become more learner-centered. The emphasis on assessment of student learning outcomes is central at most community colleges and, as Renner suggests, may help to demonstrate why service-learning is an effective vehicle for creating significant learning experiences. Renner cites concrete examples of assessment work and urges community college faculty to move beyond local knowledge. As she states, "Our expertise in community partnering and practical measures of learning are fundamental to understanding the impact of service-learning. We have a responsibility and an opportunity to contribute in a meaningful way to the research on this topic."

Chapter 5 shifts the focus from students to faculty by suggesting ways that practitioners engaged in service-learning can add to the growing knowledge of the scholarship of teaching and learning. It notes that just as students involved in service-learning gain insight into their experiences through reflection, faculty engaged in the scholarship of teaching and learning gain insight into their practice by analyzing and reflecting on student work. If faculty can begin placing the local findings they observe in classrooms within a larger framework of research, their work will have more value for the broader academic community.

Community Colleges as Service-Learning Leaders

Community colleges can make important contributions to service-learning in higher education through a deeper analysis of student learning and a clear explanation of practices for strengthening communities in and outside of classrooms. Faculty can serve as bridges between high schools and universities, as comfortable partners with the local community, and as reflective practitioners who demonstrate in concrete ways how service-learning can create transformative learning experiences for a diverse population of students. We hope this book will help them achieve all of these goals.

References

Brint, S., & Karabel, J. (1989). *The diverted dream: Community colleges and the promise of educational opportunity in America, 1900–1985.* New York: Oxford University Press.

Fink, L.D. (2003). *Creating significant learning experiences: An integrated approach to designing college courses.* San Francisco: Jossey-Bass.

Heffernan, K. (2001). *Fundamentals of service-learning course construction.* Providence, RI: Campus Compact.

Spitzberg, I.J., & Thorndike, V.V. (1992). *Creating community on college campuses.* Albany: State University of New York Press.

Zlotkowski, E., Duffy, D.K., Franco, R., Gelmon, S.B., Norvell, K.H., Meeropol, J.M., & Jones, S. (2004). *The Community's College: Indicators of engagement at two-year institutions.* Providence, RI: Campus Compact.

Chapter One

Using Service-Learning to Build Attainment Pathways

ROBERT FRANCO

A GREAT DEAL OF RECENT LITERATURE HAS FOCUSED ON the opportunities awaiting—and challenges confronting—America's community colleges. These colleges are the subject of increasing scholarly research because over the past three decades community colleges have become:

- *The fastest growing sector of American higher education,* increasing in enrollment by 375%, compared with 103% growth at public four-year colleges and 72% growth at private four-year colleges (Boswell, 2004). They enroll 11.6 million students, or 46% of all U.S. undergraduates, and the vast majority of first- and second-year students.

- *The sector that serves the most low-income students,* including the majority of college students from the lowest socioeconomic quintile (Adelman, 2005), as well as high proportions of underserved populations and first-generation college goers.

- *A key access point for students of color.* Community colleges currently enroll 47% of all African American, 55% of all Hispanic, and 57% of all Native American college students (American Association of Community Colleges, 2007).

- *A barometer of the American dream.* If, as Carnevale (2004, p. 39) states, America "emphasizes equality of educational opportunity rather than equality of economic opportunity," then for a growing number of Americans, achieving better jobs with higher incomes will increasingly be the responsibility of the community college.

- *A powerful learning nexus*—an "essential educational player in cities, counties, states and nations" (Milliron & Wilson, 2004, p. 52).

The opening and closing chapters of Campus Compact's recent book *The Community's College: Indicators of Engagement at Two-Year Institutions* (Zlotkowski et al., 2004) make a convincing case that community colleges are themselves community-based organizations rooted in urban, rural, and suburban places across the American landscape. These institutions provide access to higher education for students from the local community. They also help prepare these students for lives of social and civic responsibility and economic productivity in their local communities—as well as for transfer to universities, often in new communities. In sum, the research on which the book was based found that community colleges generally do not suffer from the town-gown stratigraphy that often afflicts other sectors of higher education. The grounding of these colleges in their communities ideally situates them to build pathways to success in both academic and community learning.

From Access to Success: Constructing Attainment Pathways

Most of the literature on community colleges discusses the numerous access-to-success issues confronting these schools. The distance from access to success has for far too long been abstracted, while millions of Americans have lost out on baccalaureate completion. A new promising direction is the formal construction of access-to-success pathways at the end of which are measurable learning outcomes.

Community colleges are now recognizing the importance of constructing "attainment pathways" (Adelman, 2005), while the Association of American Colleges and Universities' *Greater Expectations* initiative promotes the design of "purposeful pathways" from high school to college to baccalaureate success (AAC&U, 2003). Community colleges are a natural nexus in the construction of attainment pathways from high school to baccalaureate degrees. Yet significant issues currently block the development of purposeful vertical pathways from high school to two-year and from two-year to four-year colleges. At the front end of the pathway, college readiness is the issue; at the mid-point, unnecessary transfer barriers are the issue (Boswell, 2004).

Service-learning collaborations can reduce the severity of these issues as students and institutions commit to democratic dialogue and a more collaborative spirit and process of problem solving. Figure 1 (pages 8 and 9) depicts how service-learning collaborations among community colleges, four-year institutions, and high schools can create pathways both to academic success and to greater civic involvement. Developing attainment pathways is more than just working on the edges of institutional change. It involves partnering with educational pipeline partners (high schools, community partners, community colleges, universities) to construct intentional and coherent routes to educational and civic success for all of our students. These pathways clearly involve academic issues of curriculum and pedagogy, as well as student affairs issues of financial aid (e.g., work-study and service scholarships at key transitions along the pathway) and student development outcomes.

In addition to depicting how service-learning can create vertical pathways for students. Figure 1 offers funding options and student oucomes at each stage. Using electronic portfolios, student learning and development outcomes can be assessed and formatively evaluated at key transition points. Community partners and colleges can collaborate to develop new funding and strategies to sustain successful programs.

Community colleges are also creating other types of attainment pathways. For example, they are working to construct horizontal attainment pathways that support the academic and career success of adult learners returning to college from rapidly transforming labor markets. "Career lattice" models provide more customized educational support and opportunities to help returning adults learn and develop new knowledge, skills, and attitudes for greater occupational mobility. In addition, incipient attainment pathways are being considered for a new type of students referred to as "swirlers," who move into and out of colleges and communities. These may be the most disengaged learners roaming around in American higher education.

Community colleges can use service-learning to fuse attainment pathways with the community pathways of civic, workforce, and economic development. As Campus Compact's Indicators of Engagement research revealed, such a fusion will be possible only if engaged faculty work collectively to develop effective curriculum and pedagogy within supportive campus-community cultures. The following sections examine how faculty members can establish such cultures and put service-learning to work to serve multiple attainment goals.

Using Service-Learning Effectively

Service-learning is a teaching and learning method that integrates critical reflection and meaningful service in the community with academic learning, personal growth, and civic responsibility. Service-learning encourages students and faculty to be active partners with community members in building stronger communities and provides students with opportunities to develop and demonstrate:

- Newly acquired knowledge, skills, and attitudes;
- Deeper understanding and application of course content and broader appreciation of the discipline; and
- A greater understanding of their relationship and responsibility to their local, national, regional, and global communities.

A key step here is to deliberately link community, civic, and academic goals. Fortunately, a number of resources are available to help community college faculty forge these links.

Service-Learning and Civic Responsibility

In 2002, the American Association of Community Colleges (AACC) published a major work entitled *A Practical Guide to Integrating Civic Responsibility into the Curriculum* (Gottlieb & Robinson, 2002). It provides an excellent and widely used definition of civic responsibility:

FIGURE 1:

Vertical Attainment Pathways: Service-Learning on Common Ground

	Service-Learning Example: Environmental Programs	Service-Learning Example: Educational Programs	Funding Options	Student Outcomes
Baccalaureate Institutions				
Seniors	Community-based environmental research—data-driven advocacy and public policy work.	Community-based educational research—data-driven advocacy and public policy work.	Funding support for research, advocacy, and public policy work.	Coherent pathway to baccalaureate.
Juniors	Leadership in environmental stewardship—advocacy, public policy.	Leadership in developing mentoring programs for vulnerable youth—advocacy, public policy.	Funding support for coordinating reflection across undergraduate levels at the university and the local community college.	Clear understanding of the real-world applications of the major. Rich portfolio of learning and experience.
Sophomores	Leadership in environmental stewardship—project planning, implementation, partnership development. Collaboration with local community college.	Leadership in developing mentoring programs for vulnerable youth—project planning, implementation, partnership development.	Collaboration with local community college. Funds for exemplary project planning, implementation, partnership development.	Real-world experience to make clearer choice of major or profession. Foundational portfolio of learning and experience.
First-Year Students	Common environmental stewardship project for all first-year students. Collaboration with local community college.	First-year students tutor at low-income, multi-ethnic elementary, middle, and high schools. Collaboration with local community college.	Funds for coordinating reflection activities for all first-year students. Small scholarships for exemplary community college service-learning students.	Clear understanding of community as common-ground context for learning. Early portfolio explorations of majors, careers, role as citizens.

	Service-Learning Example: Environmental Programs	Service-Learning Example: Educational Programs	Funding Options	Student Outcomes

Community Colleges

Sophomores	Leadership in environmental stewardship—project planning, implementation. Collaboration with nearby university.	Leadership in developing mentoring programs for vulnerable youth—project planning, implementation, partnership development. Collaboration with nearby university.	Funds for exemplary project planning, implementation, partnership development.	2-year/4-year service-learning pathways that expedite and facilitate transfer. Real-world experience to make clearer choice of major or profession. Foundational portfolio of learning and experience.
First-Year Students	Common environmental stewardship project for all first-year students. Collaboration with nearby university.	First-year students tutor at low-income, multi-ethnic elementary, middle, and high schools. Collaboration with nearby university.	Funds for coordinating reflection activities for all first-year students. Small scholarships for exemplary high school service-learning students.	Clear understanding of community as common-ground context for learning. Early portfolio explorations of majors, careers, role as citizens.
Remedial and Developmental Students	Planning and developing campus-community recycling projects. Learning the campus as a community of caring citizens.	Remedial, developmental students tutor at low-income, multi-ethnic elementary, middle, and high schools.	Small scholarships for exemplary service-learning by remedial and developmental students.	Understanding of engagement as central to the learning-centered mission of the campus. Knowledge that they can make a positive difference for themselves and others despite initial educational under-preparedness.

High Schools

Senior and Juniors	Collaboration with community college and university on environmental stewardship and community recycling.	Seniors and juniors tutor at low-income, multi-ethnic middle schools.	Funds for travel to the National Service-Learning Conference.	Knowledge of local campuses that provide comprehensive civic engagement opportunities across the undergraduate experience.

Civic responsibility means active participation in the public life of a community in an informed, committed, and constructive manner, with a focus on the common good. (p. 16)

AACC's Horizons Service-Learning Project

"The goals of AACC's national project, Community Colleges Broadening Horizons through Service-Learning, are to build on established foundations to integrate service-learning into the institutional climate of community colleges and to increase the number, quality, and sustainability of service learning programs through an information clearinghouse, data collection and analysis, model programs, training and technical assistance, publications, and referrals."

From AACC's website. For more information, see www.aacc.nche.edu/Content/NavigationMenu/ResourceCenter/Projects_Partnerships/Current/HorizonsServiceLearningProject/HorizonsServiceLearningProject.htm

The book is based on a wide range of successful field-based models and approaches from colleges in AACC's Horizons Service-Learning Project (see the sidebar, left). Chapters on the practice and assessment of civic responsibility, as well as reflection resources and exercises and useful films, articles, and web resources, provide immediately useful and high-quality tools for the faculty member committed to civic engagement and engaged learning.

Another valuable resource is The Community College National Center for Community Engagement (CCNCCE). The organization describes itself as "a leader in advancing programs and innovations that stimulate active participation of institutions in community engagement for the attainment of a vital citizenry." CCNCCE offers training, grants, publications, and other resources for community colleges. More information about the organization and its programs is available at www.mc. maricopa.edu/other/engagement.

Developing Curricula

Campus Compact's Indicators of Engagement research identified the following successful practices in developing service-learning curricula at the department/discipline level (Zlotkowski et al., 2004, p.30):

- Enlist department chairs to encourage adoption of engaged practices throughout the department and discipline.

- Work with a community partner to organize projects around a complex community initiative.

- Partner with workforce development and other learning-based programs.

- Create forums for interdisciplinary communication and cooperation.

- Give individual faculty time to devote to service and leeway in developing service-learning initiatives.

In developing service-learning attainment pathways, these practices will provide students with multiple opportunities to learn through community work in their developmental, first-year experience, general education, and career curricula.

The Indicators research also identified the following best practices in service-learning pedagogy and epistemology (Zlotkowski et al., 2004, p. 35):

- Integrate service with academics—make it an integral part of course design.

- Ensure that credit is for learning outcomes, not good deeds.

- Define academic outcomes to include all relevant outcomes, including community development and workforce development outcomes.

- Give students latitude in choosing projects and project locations.

- Offer reflection activities to deepen learning.

- Find concrete ways to involve the community in the teaching and learning process. (For example, community partners can teach course concepts related to their civic involvement, model how individuals contribute to their communities through the problem-solving process, and expose students to resource realities for community programs.)

In developing service-learning attainment pathways, these practices can help students achieve both course and program learning outcomes that prepare them for lives as civically responsible and economic productive members of their communities.

Implementing Service-Learning

Kerrissa Heffernan's *Fundamentals of Service-Learning Course Construction* (2001) provides a comprehensive assessment and analysis of service-learning course syllabi. Although most of the syllabi were developed at four-year institutions, the key components of effective syllabi apply across all higher education sectors. According to Heffernan (p. 9), exemplary service-learning syllabi:

- Include service as an expressed goal.

- Clearly describe how the service experience will be measured and what will be measured.

- Describe the nature of the service placement and/or project.

- Specify the roles and responsibilities of students in the place and/or service project.

- Define the need(s) the service placement meets.

- Specify how students will be expected to demonstrate what they have learned in the placement/project (journal, papers, presentations).

- Present course assignments that link the placement and the course content.

- Include a description of the reflective process.

- Include a description of the expectations for the public dissemination of students' work.

Heffernan also identifies four central issues that faculty must address in developing strong service-learning courses (p. 82):

1. Engagement—Does the service component meet a public good? How do you know this? Has the community been consulted? How? How have the campus-community boundaries been negotiated, and how will they be crossed?

2. Reflection—Is there a mechanism that encourages students to link their service experience to course content and to reflect upon why the service is important?

3. Reciprocity—Is reciprocity evident in the service component? How? "Reciprocity suggests that every individual, organization, and entity involved in the service-learning functions as both a teacher and a learner. Participants are perceived as colleagues, not as servers and clients" (Jacoby, 1996).

4. Public dissemination—Is service work presented to the public or made an opportunity for the community to enter into a public dialogue? How?

As noted earlier, community colleges do not usually have the same town-gown disconnects as some four-year institutions. Community colleges are more likely to be consulting and negotiating with community partners in reciprocal relationships. Often, however, both community college and community stakeholders take insufficient time for reflecting on these relationships. A greater focus on service-learning, civic engagement, and public dissemination can promote more and deeper dialog and reflection on reciprocal partnerships and future shared goals.

Achieving Learning Outcomes

Service-learning assignments can be developed so that students demonstrate a wide range of learning outcomes, including the following:

- Written and oral communication.

- Reliability and time management.

- Critical thinking, including decision-making and problem-solving.

- Knowledge of community history and social networks.

- Ability to work in diverse teams and sensitivity to diverse clients and communities.

- Development of commitment to place.

- Willingness to learn, serve, and lead in strengthening communities.

The learning outcome assessment movement in higher education provides a powerful synergy for the rapid development of service-learning and campus-community partnerships, since the deep learning outcomes delineated above require both collective faculty work and strong community partnerships.

In *Turning to One Another,* Wheatley (2002, p. 28) argues convincingly that

> All change, even very large and powerful change, begins when a few people start talking with one another about something they care about…we rediscover a sense of unity. We remember we are part of a greater whole. And as an added joy, we also discover our collective wisdom.

Stiehl and Lewchuk, leaders in higher education learning outcomes assessment, build on Wheatley's work by emphasizing that in the learning outcomes process,

> Faculties become acutely aware of the collective nature of their responsibility for student learning outcomes and standards. And once the conversation begins, it is almost impossible to stop. Shared insights generate a multitude of questions around entry requirements, course sequencing, course alignment with intended learning outcomes, assessment strategies, basic skills needs, themes, capstone experiences, and capstone assessment. (2005, p. 3)

In this passage, Stiehl and Lewchuk identify a range of questions that need to be answered for attainment pathways to be developed and assessed. For service-learning attainment pathways to be successful, faculty and community partners must take collective responsibility for helping students learn collective responsibility.

Engaging Community College Students

Community college students are demographically diverse in many ways: ethnicity, race, income, gender, age, and disability, among others. Woven through this demographic diversity is experiential diversity, aptly and succinctly described by Mundhenk (2004, p.38):

> Heterogeneous in almost every respect, community college students are more likely to need remediation, less likely to complete a degree in a conventional timeframe, more likely to be testing out the college experience, more likely to be seeking coursework sufficient to their needs but not necessarily wanting to pursue a full program, and much more likely to have to balance education with the demands of job and family.

The effectiveness of community colleges is increasingly being measured in terms of how well these diverse students are retained in courses, persist across semesters, continue into subsequent fall semesters, complete degrees, transfer and graduate, and enter and advance in jobs and careers.

Using the Community College Survey of Student Engagement (CCSSE), community colleges are also assessing the quality of their students' experience. The rationale for using CCSSE is simple: assessing and improving the quality of the student experience will lead to improvements in institutional effectiveness outcomes.

The CCSSE assesses the student experience on five key benchmarks:

- Active and collaborative learning
- Student-faculty interaction

- Academic challenge

- Student effort

- Support for student success

Well-developed service-learning courses and attainment pathways can contribute to an enhanced student experience in a number of ways:

- Through service-learning, faculty, students, and community partners are actively engaged in collaborative course design, the learning process, and civic action.

- Service-learning offers faculty and students the time and space to reflect on both the service and the learning.

- Well-constructed service-learning assignments tap into multiple skills: they are academically rigorous, and community-based roles and responsibilities require critical thinking and effective action.

- Service-learning assignments require greater student effort to make course-community curricular connections, more student time in service to the community, and more creative energy in community problem-solving.

- Service-learning and civic engagement centers on campus provide significant support for student success by assisting with community placement, coordinating peer reflection sessions, and providing additional leadership opportunities for AmeriCorps/VISTA, work study, and dedicated service-learning students. These leaders provide a strong multiplier effect in the student support services area; 10 student leaders in the service-learning center can support hundreds of diverse service-learning students along their attainment pathways.

Fusing Academic, Career, and Community Development

Community colleges are ideally situated between high schools and universities to play a lead role in constructing successful attainment pathways. Service-learning curriculum and pedagogy can link these attainment pathways with the attainment of community, workforce, and economic development goals and objectives. Thus, service-learning can fuse student academic and career success with community and economic development.

Service-learning course and program design has continued to advance since the seminal works of Heffernan (2001) and Gottlieb and Robinson (2002). In the future, our ability to fuse courses into attainment and community pathways will depend on the ability of faculty to work collaboratively with community partners to provide learning experiences for students that link academic and civic goals. By committing to this next level of civic engagement, community college leaders can develop attainment pathways along which their diverse students will enjoy a high-quality learning experience, complete degrees, and be prepared for lives as civically responsible and economic productive members of their communities.

As a natural nexus for P-16 pathways and community and economic development locally, nationally, and globally, community colleges can catalyze ideas, issues, practices, and policies to renew civic energy, resulting in stronger citizens and communities and a resurgence in American democratic participation. America's community colleges were designed for this very purpose; service-learning is a powerful strategy for reclaiming this purpose and this promise.

References

AAC&U. (2003, Winter). Purposeful pathways? A look at school college alignment. *Peer Review, 5*(2).

Adelman, C. (2005). *Moving into town—and moving on: The community college in the lives of traditional-age students.* Washington, DC: U.S. Department of Education.

American Association of Community Colleges. (2007). *About community colleges: Fast facts.* Available at www.aacc.nche.edu/Content/NavigationMenu/AboutCommunityColleges/Fast_Facts1/Fast_Facts.htm.

Boswell, K. (2004, November/December). Bridges or barriers: Public policy and the community college transfer function. *Change, 36*(6), 22-29.

Carnevale, A. (2004). Why learning: The value of higher education to society and the individual. In K. Boswell & C.D. Wilson (Eds.), *Keeping America's promise: A report on the future of community colleges.* Denver, CO: The Education Commission of the States and the League for Innovation in the Community College.

Gottlieb, K., & Robinson, G. (2006). *A practical guide to integrating civic responsibility into the curriculum* (2nd ed.). Washington, DC: Community College Press.

Heffernan, K. (2001). *Fundamentals of service-learning course construction.* Providence, RI: Campus Compact.

Jacoby, B., & Associates. (1996). *Service-learning in higher education: Concepts and practices.* San Francisco: Jossey-Bass.

Milliron, M.D., & Wilson, C. (2004, November/December). No need to invent them: Community colleges and their place in the education landscape. *Change, 36*(6), 52–58.

Mundhenk, R. (2004, November/December). Communities of assessment. *Change, 36*(6), 36–41.

Stiehl, R., & Lewchuk, L. (2005). *The MAPPING primer: Tools for reconstructing the college curriculum.* Corvallis, OR: The Learning Organization.

Wheatley, M.J. (2002). *Turning to one another: Simple conversations to restore hope for the future.* New York: Simon & Schuster.

Zlotkowski, E., Duffy, D.K., Franco, R., Gelman, S.B., Norvell, K.H., Meeropol, J., & Jones, S. (2004). *The community's college: Indicators of engagement at two-year institutions.* Providence, RI: Campus Compact.

Best Practices for Creating Quality Service-Learning Courses

AMY HENDRICKS

T O USE SERVICE-LEARNING IN A COURSE, faculty members must make a number of decisions before ever stepping into the classroom. Initial "thought work" includes gaining a thorough understanding of the pedagogy of service-learning, as well as visualizing how service-learning will change the way the course is currently taught. This preliminary work will provide a sound basis for creating an effective service-learning course and help guide the design process.

This chapter offers a step-by-step guide to planning and implementing service-learning in the classroom, from goal setting to specific actions needed to design the course, choose a service site, determine the most effective type of service, and document and evaluate learning. Several appendices offer examples of forms covering everything from student applications to progress reports to final evaluations. Finally, a quick reference section provides 10 keys to creating a quality service-learning syllabus.

Preliminary Work

A faculty member who is considering using service-learning is his or her classes needs to think through the following issues before beginning course design.

Articulate the Reason for Service-Learning

It is important to establish and communicate why you believe a service-learning component will enhance the learning experience in your course and engage students in the civic life of their communities. If you do not fully understand why you're using service-learning, the students won't either. Be prepared not only to tell your students about the service-learning opportunity available in your course but also to explain how it will enhance your course curriculum and how they will benefit from it.

In most cases, service is optional rather than required, so you will need to make a strong case. You will no doubt view service as a great opportunity, but your savvy (and skeptical) students, who have come of age in a world geared to consumer marketing, will want proof that this is not just a way to get them to do extra work. You will need to convey to students, preferably from the first day of class, why service-learning is enriching and fulfilling and why it should be viewed as part of the class, not as an extraneous add-on. If they view it as something "extra," students will likely resist the idea.

Review your curriculum and course objectives and visualize how a service-learning component would bring these objectives to life. Many institutions use a standardized syllabus template that requires faculty to include a list of course objectives that are agreed upon by various committees and approved by the state. Not surprisingly, such lists are often dry and full of academic jargon that is foreign and unattractive to students, especially those who have not yet chosen a major. A list of course objectives is a perfect opportunity to point out to students how service-learning can enrich the course and make it more meaningful and even more fun.

Additionally, service-learning can be used to link your course objectives to the larger goal of civic engagement in the lives of college students. Student may not realize the impact that biology has on the larger community—it may seem like a lot of difficult facts and formulae, not a force for change in society. Applying the facts learned in class to a problem in the community reinforces those connections in ways that a lecture could never do.

Take, for example, a course on government. One objective in such a course is to understand the role of elections in political life: how they work, how campaigns are funded, the qualifications candidates must have in order to run, and so forth. These facts may be exciting to the professor, but many students will find them fairly dry, if not stiflingly boring. Think how much more students would learn if they were working on a campaign at the same time that they were learning about elections in class. It would not be surprising if these students found discrepancies in the textbook version and the real-life version of campaigns and elections, which could lead to insightful discussions about such subjects as the role of money, the "insider" game, the role of political party operatives, and many other aspects of campaigning that might not be covered by the book.

Think also about how these students might feel about their role as citizens after seeing the effects of their work on the campaign. These students would learn to care who got elected after seeing the power of those in office. They would likely never miss an opportunity to vote again. Just one student's experience could bring life to the entire class during class discussions. The faculty member must see these connections, believe in them, and be able to convey them to students in order to "sell" the service-learning idea.

Recognize That Service-Learning Will Change How You Teach

Using service-learning as a teaching tool means giving up control. Having students learn outside the classroom means that some of their learning will be unknown to you. You will be called upon to react to the new experiences that they bring to the class, rather than control what is distributed to them; this means that you will not be able to control the context of discussions as much as before. This change can be disturbing to an instructor used to a high degree of organization and time management in the classroom. But unless the instructor is willing to let go and grasp the "teachable moment," students' service experience will be stunted.

A newcomer to service-learning should be open to using class discussion as a tool. In most cases, you will have some students performing service and some (probably most) who are not. The key is to be prepared to let those who are performing service relate their experiences to you and the other students in an atmosphere conducive to open discussion, but one that focuses on course objectives.

Because service-learning students are likely to bring real-world dilemmas and questions back to the classroom, the answers may not always be immediately at hand. There may be times when you will have to say, "I don't know the answer to that." This is not a drawback. In fact, these moments are excellent opportunities to teach students *how to learn.* You can simply follow up by saying, "I'll find out." Students will recognize and respect the love of learning in this response.

Before using a service-learning component, faculty members should think about their own teaching and learning style and note where adjustments might have to be made in dealing with this unique learning tool.

Begin with the End in Mind

Before creating a service-learning course component, it is important to identify goals for the students in your class. This involves visualizing students who have completed the service-learning portion of the course. How will those students' learning differ from that of the students who did not participate in service-learning? While they are performing the service, what connections do you want the students to make with the material in your course? Outcomes from students include their own personal growth, career choices, social skills, and the pure academic benefit of better understanding the material (Stacey, Rice, & Langer, 1997). Perhaps most important of all, the experience will teach civic engagement.

For instance, one academic goal for veterinary technology students serving at the local Humane Society is to understand animal care more fully. But these students may also be expected to grow as members of society, better understanding their role as citizens and stewards of the ecological system in which they live. They will learn what they can and cannot expect from government, from citizen organizations, and from the general public. They will learn who needs to be educated about their subject, and why. Most important, they will understand their own ability to change society. Other goals have to do with students' personal growth: discerning whether veterinary technology is a field they truly want to work in; understanding their own social and political views in more depth; gaining experience in areas such as social interaction, diversity, and tolerance.

The goals for students should focus on both *service* and *learning*. Service to the community means that the need for the students' service and the issues addressed must be *from the community*—not something the teacher or students think up and then tell the community they will supply. This idea is linked to the concept of "ownership" in the community: the service itself is owned by, and is a reflection of, the community. The focus on learning is equally important; service with no connection to the course content is volunteerism, not service-learning. Finally, service that does not fit the needs of the student is unjustified. The student should grow from the experience as an individual and a member of society; if that goal is not being achieved, the service should be reevaluated. All of these connections between service and learning must be conceptualized before introducing the idea to the class.

This step also requires faculty members to think through the concrete aspects of the service experience they want their students to study, or at least pay careful attention to, during their service. If a psychology professor sends students to a mental health facility, for example, he or she won't be there to guide them in person. Students become their own teachers at the service site; the professor back at the college can help by supplying them in advance with guidelines and tools. In this case, students might be told to observe the psycho-social factors contributing to a patient's condition, the efficacy of certain therapies, the interaction between clients and service providers, and their own feelings when confronted with mentally ill patients.

In short, students setting out on a service experience need guidance on how to turn that service into learning. This requires vision on the part of the instructor.

Identify Support Structures

Before getting started, find out what resources are available at your institution to help you develop a service-learning course. Procedures will differ greatly depending on whether a formal service-learning center exists at your institution and, if it does, the extent of its maturity and institutionalization. The following section on course design includes a discussion of the options for supplying the "people power" necessary to create a successful service-learning course component if you do not have a formal center.

Steps in Course Design

Decide Whether Service Will Be Optional or Required

The first decision to be made is whether to require service-learning or to offer it as an option. One may question whether service work, by definition, can be "required." Service-learning is different from traditional volunteer work, however. Since the service is a tool for meeting course learning objectives, faculty members can require service in the community as part of the course as long as they have considered factors such as accommodating students with disabilities or restrictive schedules. If the course offers a variety of service sites as options, this is usually not a hindrance.

If you decide to require service-learning, it is important to make the requirement clearly known to students while they still have the chance to opt out of the course. For example, the requirement should be listed in the college catalog, the course or class webpage if available, and in the syllabus distributed on the first day of class. If a student objects to the requirement, he or she should be able to exit the class during the add/drop period at no charge. In short, the sooner this requirement is known, and in great detail, the better.

Requiring service-learning, rather than offering it as an option, allows all students in the class to share the benefits of the experience. Recently at Brevard Community College, a biology professor required her students to participate in a "Pond Legacy Project" as a part of a Fundamentals of Biology class. This course, which counts toward the science requirement for the Associate in Arts degree, is meant for non–science majors. But it's likely that this professor tempted a few students to switch majors after the experience of creating a native plant habitat around a retention pond at a nearby public park.

In this community, retention ponds are necessary to prevent flooding, so they are common, but rarely attractive or serviceable beyond their basic function. In this case, a large pond was created to store water; with students' efforts, it also became a beautiful landscape, a water-testing site, and a native wildlife habitat. The students were able to practice many learning objectives in their service-learning experience: they used GPS equipment to station water testing and planting sites, they identified native plants best suited to the habitat, and they actively participated in water testing and data analysis. In addition, they worked with local high school students assigned to the same project and were charged with coming to a consensus on the plants to incorporate, the development of a mapping system, and the actual planting of native specimens.

The students came away with Fundamentals of Biology not only in their notebooks, but also under their fingernails and in their lungs. Our college students applied the facts and formulae they learned in the classroom, but also mentored younger students from the nearby high schools, building their leadership skills. Best of all, they learned what united community members can do to make publicly owned land best serve the larger community. Every time the students or their family and friends come to the park, they feel a sense of ownership and efficacy that cannot come from any other type of college classroom experience. Whether they would have had the same sense of collective ownership in a class that offered service-learning as an option, adopted by only some students, is an open question.

Another option is to offer a "pure" or stand-alone service-learning course. Such courses are based on the pedagogy of civic engagement, and many of the hours of "class time" are spent in the community. In essence, the community is the classroom. Students are usually self-directed in their learning. Service sites can vary dramatically; they are often chosen by the students based on an agree-upon curriculum, decided by consensus during the first weeks of class. The required number of hours can vary, but 30+ hours is typical for a 16-week semester. Chapter 3 of this publication discusses stand-alone service-learning courses in greater depth.

In the community college setting, requiring community service in a class is still relatively rare. In most cases the instructor chooses to offer service-learning as an option, either to bolster a grade (extra credit on a particular assignment or on the class as a whole) or to replace a grade that can be earned by another assignment in the class (such as a paper or exam).

The Brevard Community College website features a number of helpful syllabi that discuss some attractive assignments that you might consider in determining whether to require service for a class. (See www.brevard.cc.fl.us; click on Education, then on Center for Service-Learning.)

Some examples of how to incorporate service-learning into different types of classes, drawn from actual courses, follow.

Chemistry. Students have the option to tutor K-12 science students for at least 20 hours during a semester. Those who complete the hours and a detailed journal documenting how the experience affected them academically and personally receive a 10% increase on their exam average.

Psychology. In this class, 20 hours of service in an approved service site, plus a reflective journal, may exempt the student from the comprehensive final exam. Students must serve at a social service agency that aids individuals in crisis in areas such as homelessness, drug addiction, domestic violence, poverty, mental illness, or joblessness. As this instructor puts it, "they won't remember my final exam in two years, but they will always remember what they learned from their service experience."

Veterinary Technology. A minimum of 20 hours of service at a nonprofit veterinary clinic, animal rescue, or pet therapy center, along with a reflective journal meeting exact criteria, earns the student exemption from the comprehensive final exam.

Political Science. A minimum of 15 hours of service in a government office, campaign, or nonprofit agency receiving state or federal funding, plus a detailed journal critiquing the agency based on what was learned in class, earns three extra points on the final grade.

Speech Communications. A student can serve for 15-20 hours at any community agency identified by the Center for Service-Learning, either to replace one of the required class speeches or to add 10–20 extra credit points to the final grade (student's option).

Statistics. A student can earn a 5% increase in his or her final grade by serving at least 15 hours in an approved community site and submitting a one-page statistical report. The data analysis submitted must contain at least one inferential statistical analysis performed on data related to the agency, with the research question posed by the student. Alternatively, the class as a group may perform statistical analysis for a nonprofit agency, working as a team to solve specific problems and produce usable data for the agency. This structure not only works well for the students but also provides valuable information for the agency that would otherwise be expensive to obtain.

American History. In lieu of writing a research paper or a series of book reviews, a student can participate in a service-learning experience (20 hours minimum) and complete both a daily journal and a formal reflection paper relating the value of the experience to the course and discussing how the service affected the student individually.

Introduction to Education. Prospective teachers in this class are required to spend 10 hours in a public school classroom assisting a teacher and 5 hours tutoring students. They have several service-learning options for fulfilling these requirements. For the tutoring, they can work within the school system or with a reading program; they can also work with the Big Brothers/Big Sisters program or the Junior Achievement program throughout the semester.

Identify Service Sites

The first step in identifying service sites is to identify community needs and the sites that are available to meet those needs. A number of resources can help in developing a list of sites, including the following (adapted from Stacey, Rice, & Langer, 1997):

- Your college center for service-learning

- A community-run volunteer center (many cities and counties operate such nonprofit organizations to connect citizens to agencies in need)

- The United Way

- Print or online telephone directories

- Social service agencies in your community, such as those that deal with children, the elderly, or the sick

- Hospitals and nursing homes

- School boards

- Local, state, and federal government offices

- Mental health facilities, including drug rehabilitation centers

- Child-care centers

- Neighborhood organizations, such as those focused on preventing crime, controlling litter, or building playgrounds

- Churches and other houses of worship

- Police precinct offices

- Chambers of commerce

- Area colleges and universities

The initial contact list can be compiled by the faculty member, the students, the center for service-learning at the institution, or a combination of the above. There are a number of opinions about the value of having students find the community partners to serve. To do so brings the student in contact with many groups in the community and calls upon them to discern and evaluate community need. These actions can help students build leadership and social skills and hone decision-making abilities. It also allows students to pursue their personal interests with the possible result of a better match between the learner and the community partner.

On the other hand, at least some significant guidance on the part of the instructor and/or the center for service-learning can guard against potential failure in this area. Students may not consider certain issues such as safety, liability, or special needs of the agency (such as time commitments). Some students may find the task so overwhelming that they give up on service-learning altogether. Therefore, at a minimum, guided site selection is recommended; better still is a collaborative effort to compile a list of potential sites.

Factors to consider in site selection include general appropriateness, site diversity, safety, infrastructure, and special requirements.

Appropriateness. Does the site address a legitimate community need? At first glance it may seem that any demonstrable need could be a service opportunity, but some selection criteria need to be thought through ahead of time. We have had students come up with some unusual options when left to their own devices: babysitting their younger siblings, working for no pay at their parents' business, volunteering at a lawyer's office, helping their church raise funds. It's not always easy to dismiss these options. For instance, what if the lawyer's office is hosting a fundraiser for leukemia research? What if the church uses some of its funds to feed the hungry? Can a student work on those projects and call it community service?

The key is to identify who benefits from the students' service and to identify whether the need is *public* or *private*. A public need serves the larger community and has ramifications beyond the student: rehabilitating former drug addicts at a center run by professionals benefits society; trying to help one's drug-addicted brother is private. Working for free at a for-profit business contributes to the private gain of the business owner; working at a fundraiser for cancer research benefits society. A community child-care center provides a social resource for those in need; babysitting one's siblings fills a private need within a family.

Many service sites have a connection to a specific church or faith, and you should carefully think through this issue as well. Many churches and religious groups serve the community in very meaningful ways, but if your students are doing "service" by proselytizing a specific faith, you have probably crossed a line into the private arena.

Diversity of Sites. How many sites should be among the choices for students? It may seem that the more sites you have on your list, the better. However, if students have free reign to choose from hundreds of sites you may be faced with a new set of problems. Too many different experiences may interfere with your ability to integrate student experiences into the course curriculum. It may also overwhelm students and actually turn them off to the experience.

On the other hand, too small a range of sites may not accommodate the students' interests or the learning objectives of your course. By limiting sites to a very small number, you may inadvertently exclude a group of students based on gender, ethnicity, or age. For example, if all of your sites are in low-income Latino communities, those with limited Spanish-speaking skills may shy away. Some agencies take only one gender as volunteers, such as group homes for male or female children. Other sites require a higher degree of maturity and/or time commitment, which may exclude younger students.

We recommend compiling a fairly large array of sites to accommodate many interests, students, and academic courses, but tailoring the choices for the students when arranging choices for a particular course. For instance, a mathematics instructor might give the students 10 or 15 options for sites whose experience will fit the math curriculum, but inform students that she will consider other options if the student sees a need and can relate that need to the course content. A government professor might require students to work for a local or state government agency (which can encompass dozens of sites, including public schools), but exclude other types of agencies.

Safety Issues. As in the field of medicine, the first rule of service in the community is to do no harm, either to the service-learning students or to those they serve. Safety factors are extremely important, and this is one area that may be overlooked by students if they are left to locate community partners on their own. Indeed, the agency itself may not have considered all angles of safety if they have not used volunteers or service learners to a great extent; if they're used to having only trained personnel on site the agency may not have considered what the untrained volunteer might encounter.

Consider a service-learner in a mental health facility who could be physically attacked by a patient (this has happened), or students who might be asked to operate machinery or tools, spend long hours in the sun, clear out poisonous vegetation from a park, or spend time with people who are ill. These factors do not have to exclude a site as a potential community partner, but the issues should be carefully considered both in choosing sites and in pairing particular students with sites. Who is available to supervise the students? What should the students do if faced with a challenging situation? What is the potential for harm?

Available Infrastructure. A site may have a great need for people to help them but lack the internal infrastructure to handle student workers. Questions to consider include: If the site is staffed only part-time, will students be asked to fill in the gaps? Does the site have staff who can effectively train, supervise, and evaluate students? Is anyone available to document the hours students have served or sign off on the project they have completed?

Some agencies with the most pressing needs cannot handle these challenges. Again, this does not mean that they should be eliminated as potential sites, but some adjustments might have to be made in the kind of service offered. For instance, instead of on-site placement, students may be able to carry out a project or create a product for the agency. A microeconomics class might prepare a model budget for a nonprofit agency that deals with abandoned animals, or a mass media class could produce a short ad for a group advocating litter control. These activities can be done in the classroom, either by the entire class or by individuals.

Special Requirements. Finally, one must ask whether the sites have any special requirements, such as mandatory training or a required time commitment. Some agencies require extensive training (such as a guardian ad litum program) and naturally do not want their newly trained helpers to contribute only a few hours of service and then leave. Some agencies, particularly those dealing with children, require fingerprinting and background checks; some require drug tests; some are physically demanding or cannot accommodate those with disabilities; some require a high level of maturity, such as sites that deal with clients' sensitive personal information.

All of these considerations must be taken into account when devising the list of sites. A separate file should be kept on each site with contact information and any special needs to help best match the site with the course and with the individual student.

Decide on the Type of Service

Once the sites are determined, it's time to decide on the parameters of the service the students can and should provide. Options to consider include short-term service, ongoing service, and class projects.

Short-Term Service. Short-term or one-time service requires less time commitment than other options but can have a big impact, and can often serve to pique the interest of a student who is only marginally attracted to the idea of community service. These short-term commitments are aimed at achieving a specific goal, including increasing public awareness of an issue, completing a task, or creating a product. Examples include building a wildlife habitat with a local nonprofit agency, painting a mural at a community center, working on a political campaign, or compiling an oral history project.

Some short-term projects bring together people from across the community, or even the state or region. Examples include one-day "Into the Street" projects, Habitat for Humanity building projects, "Adopt a Road" projects, fundraisers for specific causes such as medical research, and public service fairs or festivals. These types of short-term projects provide opportunities for students to serve the community and become acquainted with community needs in a short amount of time.

Ongoing Service or Placement. Placement at an agency implies that the student will serve over a period time that can extend indefinitely, with the student returning to the site on a regular basis, usually a few hours per week. These placements are probably the most typical form of service-learning work. Students can tutor young children in the America Reads program, serve as a Big Brother or Big Sister, volunteer in a hospice organization, aid an elementary school teacher, care for animals at the Humane Society, or choose one of thousands of other options. It is not uncommon for a student to begin by committing to the minimum number of hours required for class credit (such as 20 hours over a semester) but continue long afterwards when bonds are forged with the agency and those it serves.

A Class Project or Product. The instructor also may elect to engage the entire class in a service-learning project as part of the course requirement or as extra credit. In this case the class works as a team to complete a project within the confines of the classroom. For instance, students in one state and local government class wrote a guidebook to their county government. The class devised the sections to be covered and did the research and writing in groups. The resulting product was distributed to local libraries and schools for use by members of the public. In another example, a graphic design class designed a brochure for a local animal adoption agency. In a third case, a statistics class performed various analyses for a nonprofit agency that would otherwise have had to contract out the work at significant cost. In all of these cases the students learned volumes about the assigned material while serving the community, and they did not have to leave the classroom to do it.

These are just some examples of how service can be defined. Combinations of the above categories also exist, as do any number of variations on the general theme.

Determine the Level of Service

To determine how service will be calculated into a course grade, the instructor must first decide on the minimum level of service. With a project or product, it is the outcome that is graded, not necessarily the time spent in service (although in some cases it is also appropriate to document time). With an ongoing placement, students need to document the hours they serve. In either case, someone at the placement site should oversee the student and sign off on the service completed (e.g., project/product completion, number of hours served).

One option in determining the appropriate number of hours to be served in a placement situation is to estimate the time that would be spent on other assignments in the class, such as the time it would take to prepare for tests or the time typically needed to research and write a term paper. We have found that about 20 hours in a 16-week semester is a good starting point. Students often continue service far beyond this mark, perhaps because after 20 hours of service they feel vested in the agency, having developed connections with people at the site and institutional knowledge of the service the agency provides. On the other hand, 20 hours is very doable for most students since it requires only 1–2 hours per week on average.

What is critical in this process is obtaining the best possible fit between the *needs of the community partner*, the *type of project* (short-term, ongoing, class project), the *needs of the student,* and the *course objectives.* The first thing to determine is community need. All service must stem from that question. The type of service provided and the hours required should match the characteristics and needs of the community partner. Next, ask how students will benefit, academically and otherwise. What will they gain from this experience? How does this experience fit the objectives of the course?

One way to find the answers to these questions is to measure the agency's expectations. A useful resource for this purpose is a "Community Service-Learning Job Description" (see Appendix 2A at the end of this chapter). This job description asks the community partner to identify key information about service positions available:

- Qualifications required (e.g., minimum age, physical requirements, background checks, etc.)
- Duties and responsibilities
- Time commitment expected
- Type of orientation required/provided
- Benefits for students
- Open-ended comments

Asking these pertinent questions is the first step in identifying best possible fit.

Communicate with the Agency

As in all aspects of social interaction, communication is critical to establishing realistic expectations on both sides. Again, the "Community Service-Learning Job Description" is a good place to start. Establishing regular and structured communication between the student, the agency, and the faculty member is key. Following are some ideas for how to manage this important area.

Define Expectations in Writing. At our institution, service-learning students and the agencies at which they serve sign a "Mutual Expectations Agreement" (see Appendix 2B, part of the form entitled "Placement Confirmation"). By signing this document, the agency commits to provide the following:

- An accurate position description, training, and assistance
- Supervision, feedback, and evaluation of the student
- Respect for the individual and learning needs of the student
- Meaningful tasks related to the student's learning objectives
- Appreciation and recognition of the student's contributions
- A safe and appropriate working environment

In return, the student commits to do the following:

- Perform duties to the best of his or her ability
- Adhere to the agency's rules and policies, including confidentiality
- Be open to supervision and instruction
- Meet time and duty commitments, or provide notice when that is not possible

When both parties sign this contract they are made to understand the seriousness of their mutual commitment (we advocate using this strong term). This type of written agreement can relieve a great deal of misunderstanding down the road. Along with the job description, this document goes a long way to define expectations and relieve uncertainty.

Establish the Means and Frequency of Communication among All Parties. It is possible to head off issues about student performance with a good means of open communication. It is important to identify a specific contact person at the agency and at the college (whether a faculty member, someone from the service-learning center, or both). A schedule of communication should be established as well. This can be formalized, as in a weekly or monthly written communication, or it can be as simple as the faculty member picking up the phone and asking the agency representative how students are doing. Better yet, the faculty member can visit the site during service hours and see and hear how the students are doing.

Likewise, students should be made aware of opportunities to communicate with the agency supervisors and their instructors. Make sure to ask questions about their service during the semester. A good way to do this is to ask during class time, which can prompt students to share some details about their site with the class.

It is especially valuable for the agency representative to evaluate the student's service in writing. The comments of the agency become a part of the student's service-learning record and can even serve as a part of a resume to help a job-seeking student demonstrate skills and work attitude. The following section discusses documentation that can aid in this process. (Note: most of the forms we use come in duplicate or triplicate; students get a copy for their own records.)

Document Service

A record of service is important for a number of reasons:

- It provides data on the impact of service-learning (number of students placed, community partners/members reached, hours served, etc.). This helps prove efficacy to the college administration and may strengthen the case for the award of grants and hard money in the annual budget.

- It provides a means of establishing student recognition for use in awarding scholarships, graduation honors, or other special recognition.

- It provides a record of accomplishment for the student to keep.

- It helps faculty members and/or the center for service-learning monitor the fit between students and community partners.

- It helps community partners understand how best to use service-learning students to achieve their goals

- It guides students in identifying their goals for academic and personal growth while practicing service-learning.

The service-learning center—or, in the absence of a formal center, the faculty member organizing the service—should keep a file on each student who applies to be a service-learner with his or her record of service while at the college. Roger Henry, in his chapter of *Successful Service-Learning Programs* (1998), suggests that student applications be organized using the following rubric:

- *Pending:* Student has applied and is waiting for placement confirmation

- *Referred:* Student has an appointment with the agency or a date set for orientation

- *Placed:* Student has formally committed to an agency and is doing community work

- *Canceled:* Student never began service assignment

- *Closed:* Student began service project but did not complete required service

- *Completed:* Student has completed service commitment

Our institution uses a series of forms to document placement, hours served (or project completed), evaluation of service, and other aspects of the service-learning experience. Appendices C through H of this chapter provide examples for your reference and use. Following are brief descriptions to help guide your choices in using this type of documentation. (Additional forms for stand-alone service-learning courses appear in Chapter 3.)

Student Application Form (Appendix 2C). The first step for a student interested in service-learning is to fill out an application form. This form is used for basic reference and contact information and opens the student file. Ideally a staff member at a service-learning center will interview the student at the time he or she submits an application form.

Student Service-Learning Status Form (Appendix 2D). The Center for Service-Learning at Brevard gives this document to faculty members 3–4 weeks into a regular (16-week) semester. They are asked to circulate it in their classes to determine what service-learning projects students are already participating in or are interested in participating in. These lists help the Center maintain an accurate database of students who have been placed and who need to be placed. It also serves as a way to remind students that there is still time to participate in service-learning.

Mid-Semester Progress Report (Appendix 2E). This form is a great means of communicating with the agency about the staff's impression of the students. By asking about key traits such as dependability, initiative, and attitude, it also serves as an excellent method by which to head off possible problems before they become significant.

Hour Report/SHOAT Verification and Final Evaluation (Appendix 2F). This form documents the hours served in an ongoing placement. SHOAT stands for Service Hours On Academic Transcript. At our institution all hours that a student serves in the community that are documented through the Center for Service-Learning are recorded on the student's academic transcript, right next to the cumulative GPA. For instance, at the end of a student's transcript you might see the following:

> *Degree Awarded:* Associate of Arts
> *Cumulative GPA:* 3.75
> *Community Service-Learning Hours Completed:* 82

The Hour Report/SHOAT Verification Form is the formal instrument through which the Center keeps track of each student's hours and conveys those hours to the registrar. Hours are documented daily or weekly and signed off on by the agency or project supervisor. At the end of the service period (usually at the end of the semester), the supervisor signs form to verify the total number of hours worked.

Equally important, the supervisor evaluates the student on the quality of service provided (from "needs help" to "excellent") using six criteria:

- Attendance

- Dependability

- Responsibility

- Initiative

- Attitude

- Cooperation

The supervisor is also invited to add open-ended comments, and we've found that they typically do spend the time to give thoughtful (and usually very positive) feedback about their student workers.

The faculty member, the student, and the Center for Service-Learning all receive copies of this document. Faculty members usually receive it from the students in the last few weeks of the semester; it's always a special moment when students proudly present evidence of what they've been doing outside of class all term. We try to spend some extra time with students on that day going over their evaluation with them. This often elicits an enthusiastic discussion from the students about what they learned at the service site.

Student Service-Learning Questionnaire (Appendix 2G). Faculty members receive this form to distribute to each of their service-learning students toward the end of the semester. The form asks students a series of questions about their experience and how it has affected them personally: in their choice of major, their career plans, their grades, their understanding of the course material, and their attitude towards the community, among other things. It also asks them to rate the effectiveness of the Center for Service-Learning. This information is used to improve the program, but also to demonstrate the return on investment in service-learning. We have learned that our program improves retention as well as having an impact on career choice and students' personal attitudes.

Evaluate Learning

An important piece of service-learning is to determine how learning will be measured when it is taking place outside of "regular" class. How do you know whether your students are meeting the course objectives through their service? How do you know whether they are gaining personal insights, knowledge of the community, and awareness of their own role in the community? Talking to them periodically can reveal a great deal, but something more formal and reliable is necessary.

The course should include a means of reflection—a method by which students can evaluate what they have gained from their service experience, both personally and as it relates to the course objectives. A great variety of reflection exercises are available, such as writing, group discussion, and even visual art projects. The key is that the faculty member needs to guide the reflection (it is, after all, just as much a part of the class as tests and term papers), and the reflection should produce a tangible result that the faculty member can evaluate.

Some evaluation tools that we have found effective include journals or essays, presentations, and tangible projects.

A Journal or Essay. Students sometimes balk at writing, but their reflection journals and essays are often stunning. We recommend guiding the student but making this assignment significantly less structured than a research assignment. In urging students to connect what they've learned to the course objectives, you might ask them to answer pointed questions in the journal or essay: Whom did the community partner you worked with serve? What were the significant social problems confronted by the agency? What do you think are the causes of these problems? What did you do to affect this issue? What more could have been done? What impediments do you see before this agency in its quest to improve the community? Questions such as these prompt students to go beyond a simple explanation of the duties and tasks they performed.

A Speech or Presentation to the Class. Just as much preparation and creativity can go into an oral presentation as into an essay or journal. One option is for several students who served at the same site to present together, contrasting and comparing their experiences or perceptions. Student might present their findings in the form of an organized class discussion or debate, asking the class to participate in their learning. They might even bring to class a person who was served by the agency, or (with the person's permission), details from his or her personal story.

A Tangible Product or Project. Some examples of a product include a promotional video or brochure created by a media class, an educational puppet show performed at a children's center, the eradication of non-native plant species in a public park, and repair of old air conditioning units at a senior center. In all of these cases, students should be asked to express what they learned from completing the project or creating the product.

How the instructor incorporates this experience into the final grade is an individual decision. Examples were given earlier in this chapter, but some options include offering extra credit on the final grade (e.g., 20 hours of service and a five-page journal garners five extra points on the final grade), accepting the service-learning component in lieu of a comprehensive final exam, or accepting service-learning in lieu of another assignment in the class, such as a paper or speech.

Troubleshoot Problems

Following is a list of possible critical incidents or concerns that might arise with a service-learning placement:

- The student does not contact his or her service site.

- The student makes initial contact and/or visits the site, but no one from the college calls to see whether the visit was a success.

- The student makes one visit but doesn't go back and there is no communication from either the student or the agency.

- Logistical impediments (time commitments, travel, agency fit) result in an unsatisfactory placement.

- Orientation is too time-consuming, too minimal, or does not seem to apply to academic work.

- The student or the agency fails to plan adequately.

- Lack of appreciation for each service-learning role—that of the student, the agency supervisor, or the college facilitator—leads to resentment.

- Lack of understanding or recognition of others' perspectives, cultural differences, or values causes misunderstandings.

- Over-concern about liability on part of the agency, program, or student interferes with the ability to get work done.

- The agency is over-concerned about students' maturity and ability to maintain confidentiality and professionalism.

- The agency needs/wants student workers but has no support structure in place.

- The agency sees students as free labor pool and assigns them to tasks that are inappropriate, not meaningful, or outside their abilities.

- Students become "crunched" at certain times of the semester (mid-terms, finals, term paper time) and service falls off.

- After a period of time in placement, the student becomes disenchanted and loses interest.

- Students suffer end-of-semester burnout, including concern about grades, time constraints, and uncertainty about how to end the relationship with the agency.

- The agency does not provide evaluation and feedback on the service experience.

Being prepared for these issues is the key to working around them. At times the problem may simply be a bad match between the student and agency, and the solution is to terminate it. At other times a phone call or email will clear up the problem instantly. There are no pat answers as every situation is unique, but good communication between the agency, the faculty member, the center, and the student is the best way not only to head off problems but also to clear the air when they arise.

Staff for Success

Now the key question: How can you get all of this done? A great deal of activity must take place to produce a quality experience for the students and the community partner. This section offers two perspectives: how to accomplish this activity through a center for service-learning, and how to solicit help from others if you do not have a formal center.

Following is a list of activities that a service-learning center may be able to perform. Note that this list is comprehensive; even a mature center is unlikely to be able to do every task. Therefore, use this list as a goal and build the program as you gain expertise, staff, contacts, and, especially, budget.

Activities that a service-learning center may be able to perform:

- Student placement (identification of sites; management of safety and legal issues; tracking of sites' capacity, hours of operation, need, clients served, and appropriateness for college students; formatting of options for student access).

- Contact with individual instructors about appropriate sites for their courses.

- Background checks for students, where appropriate.

- Training, where necessary.

- Assistance for students, faculty, and community agencies when questions or problems arise.

- Record keeping (placements, hours served, evaluation).

- Contact with Admissions/Registration to document hours on transcripts.

- Recognition (events, certificates, awards) for all stakeholders.

- Facilitation of reflection activities.

- Provision of readings and assignments that can be used in multiple disciplines.

- Continued contact with community partners to reassess needs of the agency and community on an ongoing basis.

- Gathering of information from community agencies to facilitate evaluation of student performance.

- Awarding of scholarships to students.

- Publicity for the service-learning program, both internally (for faculty, staff, administration, students) and externally (for community members, media); creation of publications, brochures, articles, annual reports.

- Recruitment of new faculty to create service-learning course components, including provision of literature, models, and other information.

• Distribution of stipends to faculty who develop new courses.

If you do not have a center for service-learning, these tasks will fall to the staff and faculty members who run the program, hopefully with some release time from their other duties. This may seem overwhelming, but remember that services need not be on the scale indicated above.

Several options exist for soliciting help from other sources. If the facilitator can obtain control of some scholarship hours, these can be awarded to students who assist in setting up and maintaining the program. Student assistants, employed by the college and assigned to particular departments or faculty members, can serve in the same capacity. It is even possible to use graduate assistants from partnering universities, especially those conducting research in the area of community involvement or social work. Finally, the agencies themselves that are seeking assistance from the college may be able to conduct some of these tasks.

Ten Keys to Creating a Quality Service-Learning Syllabus

We conclude with a short summary of ten key characteristics of an effective service-learning course component. The syllabus is the most important course document the student will receive during the semester, conveying the faculty member's hopes and expectations for the course. When it comes to service-learning, the syllabus is especially important as a means of explaining why the program is offered and what the benefits are to the student and to the class as a whole.

As Heffernan (2001) notes, however, it's not easy to clearly convey the meaning and function of service-learning to students in a syllabus. She found that many service-learning syllabi were "overwhelming and confusing" and that they could easily be full of "gaps, leaps, and assumptions" (p. iii). The following tips do not purport to provide all of the answers about writing a good syllabus, but they should serve as a guide in creating a clear and effective document.

1. An effective service-learning syllabus includes a clear definition of service-learning. Students often confuse service-learning and volunteerism or do not understand how academics are tied to the experience. A crisp one-sentence explanation should be front and center in describing the course content. Here is an example from a Brevard Community College course on Fundamentals of Speech Communication, taught by Dr. Nancy Arnett: "Service-learning is a method by which students learn and develop through active participation in thoughtfully organized service experiences that enhance what is taught at the college by extending student learning beyond the classroom." It is useful to include concrete examples that relate to your specific course.

2. An effective service-learning syllabus explains how the service experience is relevant to the curriculum and to the goals of civic engagement. The instructor should convey to students what components of the course the service experience will reinforce or enhance. Here is one example from a history course: "History is not just about 'old dead white guys,' or a list of dates floating in space. It is about ordinary people who, through the course of living their lives, made history. What better way, then, to learn history than to live it through service to the community in which one lives?"

3. An effective service-learning syllabus describes the role of the center for service-learning (if applicable). The syllabus should include the physical location of the office and the services it provides. If the center is well-equipped and the requirements are explained in the syllabus, it should be possible to tell students to "take this syllabus, go to the center, and tell them you want to do service-learning." Depending on the center's capabilities, students may need no further instruction to get started.

4. An effective service-learning syllabus clearly explains the student placement process. Students should be told where to go to initiate the process, what sites are appropriate and available, and how to make initial contact with the placement site. A service-learning center that is fairly advanced can inform students of the choice of sites available for that class. If you are working on your own, you'll need to provide students with a list of suitable agencies or service projects. In either case there should be some direction in the syllabus as to what steps the student should take in the short term.

5. An effective service-learning syllabus specifies the time commitment involved for the student. This includes not only the minimum required hours at the service site but also the time required to complete related activities such as seminars, reports, or class presentations. You may also want to include a disclaimer about travel time, required training, background checks, or fingerprinting, if those items apply.

6. An effective service-learning syllabus delineates deadlines and due dates for placement, completion of required hours, and submission of related assignments. Because the service is part of the course, these deadlines should be included in the comprehensive class calendar—the same document that lists due dates for papers, projects, and exams. Some instructors include an additional hand-out that fully explains the service-learning component. It is important that students have this at the beginning of the course.

> ### Learning by Example
>
> When seeking to create a service-learning syllabus, one of the best places to start is to find examples of what others have done. Try asking colleagues what has worked for them. Many print and online resources also offer examples, including Campus Compact's searchable online database of service-learning syllabi, available at www.compact.org/syllabi.

7. An effective service-learning syllabus explains what service site and/or college documentation is required for successful completion of the service component. Ideally, all parties—the agency or project supervisor, the student, the faculty member, and the service-learning center, should have copies of all required forms. In some cases these forms come from the center; in others the faculty member provides them. Either way, plan to have replacements on hand for copies that get lost.

8. An effective service-learning syllabus specifies how the student's experience will be evaluated. Students should understand how the experience is factored into his or her class grade: as extra credit, in lieu of another assignment, as a required assignment, etc. If the points are variable (e.g., "up to 5 points of extra credit may be assigned"), students should know the criteria for assignment of points.

9. An effective service-learning syllabus explains how to address problems that may arise with the placement. Potential problems may include student dissatisfaction with the placement site, scheduling conflicts, personal conflicts, unmet expectations, interruptions in the service commitment, or delays in the placement process, among other challenges. If there is no center for service-learning at the college, the faculty member should be prepared to handle these problems.

10. An effective service-learning syllabus includes a reflection component with clear and specific goals, which may include intellectual, civic, ethical, cross-cultural, career-related, or other goals. Will this reflection happen within the class, outside of class, online, or in some other forum? Some of the many options for reflection include a written journal, essay, or research paper; a multimedia presentation; a one-on-one seminar; a group discussion; or a play, film, or music production. The ways that students can express what they have learned are unlimited; the key is to identify and structure these methods to guide students in expressing themselves.

With these structures and processes in place, you should be well prepared to offer students a service-learning program that will enhance their college experience in multiple ways.

References

Heffernan, K. (2001). *Fundamentals of service-learning course construction.* Providence, RI: Campus Compact.

Henry, R. (1998). *Community college and service-learning: A natural at Brevard Community College.* In E. Zlotkowski (Ed.), Successful service-learning programs: New models of excellence in higher education (pp. 81–108). Bolton, MA: Anker Publishing Company, Inc.

Stacey, K., Rice, D., & Langer, G. (1997). *Academic service-learning: Faculty development manual.* Ypsilanti, MI: Eastern Michigan University, Office of Academic Service-Learning.

Appendix 2A

Community Service-Learning Job Description

NAME OF AGENCY

DATE

ADDRESS

TELEPHONE

NAME OF SUPERVISOR

SERVICE COORDINATOR

TELEPHONE

SERVICE POSITION/JOB TITLE

Qualifications

Duties/Responsibilities

Number of Students Needed

Minimum Time Commitment

Starting/Ending Date

Training Requirement/Schedule

Orientation/Schedule

Comments/Benefits

Appendix 2B

Placement Confirmation Form

STUDENT NAME

COMMUNITY PARTNER PLACEMENT SITE

SUPERVISOR OR COORDINATOR

DUTIES

DAYS AND HOURS

STARTING DATE   ENDING DATE

STUDENT IS WORKING AS COMMUNITY SERVICE-LEARNER :   YES   NO

Mutual Expectations Agreement

I. Community Partner/Placement Site—We commit to the following:

- To provide an adequate position description, orientation/training, and assistance to the student service-learner
- To provide supervision, feedback, and evaluation on student performance
- To respect the individual and learning needs of the student
- To provide meaningful tasks related to skills, interests, and learning objectives
- To provide appreciation and recognition of the student's contributions
- To provide a safe and appropriate working environment

II. Community Service-Learner—I commit to the following:

- To perform my respective duties to the best of my ability
- To adhere to organizational rules, procedures, and policies, including the confidentiality of organization and client information
- To be open to supervision with mutual feedback that will facilitate service-learning growth
- To meet time and duty commitments or, if I cannot attend, to provide adequate notice so that alternative arrangements can be made

III: Agreed to:

COMMUNITY PARTNER/ PLACEMENT SITE SIGNATURE   DATE

COMMUNITY SERVICE-LEARNING STUDENT SIGNATURE   DATE

Distribution: White (Faculty Member)   Yellow (CSL)   Pink (student)

Appendix 2C

Service-Learning Student Application Form

DATE

NAME   STUDENT NUMBER   BIRTHDAY (DAY/MONTH)

ADDRESS

EMAIL ADDRESS   PHONE

OPTIONAL:

The following information is important to match/place service-learning students with community service sites (some service sites have minimum age requirements or gender-specific requests):

GENDER: ❏ Male ❏ Female   AGE: ❏ 15–17 ❏ 18–20 ❏ 21 and over

ETHNIC GROUP (for reporting purposes only):

❏ Asian/Pacific Islander   ❏ Native American/Alaskan Native ❏ Black (Not Hispanic Origin)
❏ Hispanic   ❏ White (Not Hispanic Origin)   ❏ Other

Will you need any accommodations with your service-learning placement because of a disability?
❏ Yes   ❏ No

ACADEMIC MAJOR/CAREER INTENT   DATE OF GRADUATION (EXPECTED)

CLASS LEVEL/EDUCATION
❏ Freshman (0–29 credit hours)   ❏ Sophomore (30 or more credit hours)
❏ Dual Enrollment   ❏ Early Admission   ❏ A.A.
❏ A.S.   ❏ B.A.   ❏ Master's   ❏ Other

ARE YOU SERVING TO SATISFY ACADEMIC CREDIT AND/OR COURSE OPTIONS?
❏ Yes   ❏ No

NAME OF COURSE(S)   INSTRUCTOR(S)

PREVIOUS SERVICE WORK OR SKILLS AND INTERESTS

HOURS PER WEEK YOU WANT TO SERVE

LIST THE DAYS AND TIMES YOU ARE AVAILABLE

WHERE WOULD YOU LIKE TO SERVE, IN ORDER OF CHOICE

1.

2.

OFFICE USE ONLY
PROGRAM REFERRAL

1ST	2ND
STAFF INITIALS DATE	STAFF INITIALS DATE
COMMENTS	COMMENTS

Appendix 2D

Student Service-Learning Status Form

Please circulate to students who are participating or interested in a service-learning experience. Return to the Center for Service-Learning on your campus for follow-up and action. This will enhance our ability to place and to track your service-learners. THANK YOU!

CLASS	INSTRUCTOR/DATE

STUDENTS: Please fill out your name, phone number, the status of your placement (REFERRED, PLACED, NOT PLACED), and the service organization site in which you are working or would like to work. If you need a new referral or any assistance from our office, please let us know what we can do for you. We will be glad to help!

*If you haven't filled out an application please come to the service-learning office ASAP.

STUDENT NAME/PHONE	VOLUNTEER ORGANIZATION/PROJECT	REFERRED	PLACED	NOT PLACED

Appendix 2E

Mid-Semester Progress Report

STUDENT NAME	TODAY'S DATE
SUPERVISOR'S NAME	SUPERVISOR'S SIGNATURE
EVALUATION PERIOD (DATES)	SERVICE HOURS TO DATE

COMMUNITY PARTNER/SERVICE SITE INFORMATION
NAME   TELEPHONE

	NEEDS HELP	AVERAGE	GOOD	EXCELLENT	CANNOT RATE
PUNCTUALITY: Gets to work on time	❏	❏	❏	❏	❏
DEPENDABILITY: Prompt; trustworthy; follows directions; meets obligations	❏	❏	❏	❏	❏
ADAPTABILITY: Catches on fast; follows detailed instructions; can switch jobs	❏	❏	❏	❏	❏
ABILITY TO GET ALONG: Cooperative; well mannered; social and emotional stability	❏	❏	❏	❏	❏
ATTITUDE: Enthusiastic; a good team worker; willing to cooperate; desires to improve	❏	❏	❏	❏	❏
INITIATIVE: Ability to work without supervision; self-motivating	❏	❏	❏	❏	❏
ABILITY TO ACCEPT SUGGESTIONS: Eager to improve; seeks assistance; follows through	❏	❏	❏	❏	❏

Do you think this individual is performing
well at this stage of the program?   ❏ YES   ❏ NO

Comments: (use back of paper if needed)

Appendix 2F Community Service-Learning Hour Report/ SHOAT Verification

Please use this form to record the number of community service-learning hours per week. **This report should be initialed weekly by your agency supervisor. At the end of your commitment, the placement site supervisor verifies total hours and completes the Student Evaluation.** See bottom of form for distribution.

Student Name:

Community Partner Name:

Student Number:

Partner Telephone #:

Faculty Instructor(s):

Supervisor's Name:

Type of Activity:
- ☐ Human Service Experience (1 credit)
- ☐ Service-Learning Option
- ☐ Community Involvement (3 credits)
- ☐ Student Organization/Club (Service Activity)
- ☐ Field Study (1 credit)
- ☐ Internship
- ☐ Volunteer

Date	M	T	W	R	F	S	S	Total # Hours	Supervisor's Initials

Date	M	T	W	R	F	S	S	Total # Hours	Supervisor's Initials

Final Student Evaluation (Organization/Placement Site completes)

OVERALL PERFORMANCE	NEEDS HELP	AVERAGE	GOOD	EXCELLENT	CANNOT RATE
Attendance:					
Dependability:					
Responsibility:					

OVERALL PERFORMANCE	NEEDS HELP	AVERAGE	GOOD	EXCELLENT	CANNOT RATE
Initiative:					
Attitude:					
Cooperative:					

Overall Evaluation of Performance and Comments:

VERIFICATION: I certify that the above information and following total completed hours are correct: **TOTAL HOURS**

Community Partner Supervisor's Signature _____ Date

Student's Signature _____ Date

Official Use Only:

Date Received: _____ Verbal Verification Date: _____ Input by: _____

CS-004 Q2000 P0706 R0706 3pt NCR DISTRIBUTION: White (Faculty Member) Yellow (CSL) Pink (Student)

Appendix 2G Student Service-Learning Questionnaire

Date:

Please take a few minutes to answer. Your answers and comments will be anonymous. When completed, return to your instructor or the Center for Service-Learning Office on your campus.

How long have you performed service?

❒ One semester   ❒ Two semesters   ❒ More

Community Partner(s)/Service Site(s) at which you have participated this semester:

1   2.

3.   4.

Did your service-learning work have any effect on your major selection? (Mark only one box.)

❒ Confirmed selection   ❒ Made me think about a new major

❒ Had no effect   ❒ Changed my major selection

Was your service-learning work recommended or required by any academic unit or professor?

❒ Yes   ❒ No

In what way did your service-learning experience affect your career plans? (Mark only one box.)

❒ Questioned my previous choice   ❒ Confirmed my plans

❒ Changed career plans   ❒ No effect

My service-learning experience is (was)… (Mark only one box.)

❒ More educational than my classroom work

❒ Equally educational with my classroom work

❒ Less educational than my classroom work

Did you receive enough help, support, and guidance from…

	YES	NO
The Center's staff?	❒	❒
Faculty sponsor?	❒	❒
Community partner supervisor?	❒	❒

Comments:

_____

_____

_____

Please rate the services provided by the Center for Service-Learning. Mark only one per row.

VS = Very Satisfied   S = Satisfied   D = Dissatisfied   VD = Very Dissatisfied   NA= Not Applicable

	VS	S	D	VD	NA
1. Helpfulness of office staff	❒	❒	❒	❒	❒
2. Service documentation and reflection materials	❒	❒	❒	❒	❒
3. Adequate orientation	❒	❒	❒	❒	❒
4. Application process	❒	❒	❒	❒	❒
5. Cooperation, friendliness of staff	❒	❒	❒	❒	❒
6. Amount, quality of communication with office	❒	❒	❒	❒	❒
7. Project, agency information provided	❒	❒	❒	❒	❒

How well were you able to integrate your practical experience with your classroom work?

❒ Not at all   ❒ Somewhat   ❒ Adequately   ❒ More than adequately   ❒ Very Well

Please rate your experience at the service site at which you participated. Mark only one per row.

	VS	S	D	VD	NA
1. Helpfulness of community partner site staff	❒	❒	❒	❒	❒
2. Adequate orientation/training	❒	❒	❒	❒	❒
3. Adequate supervision	❒	❒	❒	❒	❒
4. Meaningful tasks to perform	❒	❒	❒	❒	❒
5. Acceptance and support	❒	❒	❒	❒	❒
6. Recognition for my efforts	❒	❒	❒	❒	❒

Overall, how would you rate your experience as a service-learner? (Mark only one.)

❒ Excellent   ❒ Good   ❒ Fair   ❒ Poor

Did your service-learning experience have at least a moderate effect on the following?
Please mark as many as apply.

- ❑ a. Future course selection?
- ❑ b. Improved GPA?
- ❑ c. Positive attitude toward academic studies/other classes?
- ❑ d. Better relationships with faculty members?
- ❑ e. Desire to stay in college or complete degree?
- ❑ f. Acquisition of specific academic skills and knowledge?
- ❑ g. Positive attitude toward "experiential" programs like this one?
- ❑ h. Positive attitude toward community involvement/citizenship?
- ❑ i. Positive attitude toward the college?
- ❑ j. Improved self-confidence?
- ❑ k. Ability to work and learn independently?
- ❑ l. Insight into your personal strengths and weaknesses?
- ❑ m. Sense of personal achievement?
- ❑ n. Sense of social responsibility or commitment to public/human service?
- ❑ o. Ethical/moral development?
- ❑ p. Development of functional life skills, e.g., communication, assertiveness, problem solving?
- ❑ q. Development of occupational skills?
- ❑ r. Understanding of social/cultural differences?
- ❑ s. Application of classroom knowledge?
- ❑ t. Enriched classroom learning?
- ❑ u. Increased desire to help or care for others?
- ❑ v. Knowledge of your community?

If you have a disability, did it impact your ability to fulfill your service-learning experience?

❑ Yes   ❑ No
If so, how?

_____

_____

What has your service-learning experience meant to you?

_____

_____

Thank you for making a difference!

Chapter Three

Stand-Alone Service-Learning Courses and Models

MARINA BARATIAN

STAND-ALONE OR "PURE" SERVICE-LEARNING COURSES are not rooted in a particular discipline but instead have service or civic engagement as their primary focus. These courses present a unique educational venue, giving students (with support from faculty) the opportunity to create a customized experience that is relevant to their personal needs and goals. Some students feel connected to specific populations or issues for personal reasons. For example, a student may volunteer at the American Cancer Society because that disease has claimed a family member. Others may have a more general interest in serving.

Regardless of students' motivation, allowing the class to be student-driven gives maximum latitude to pursue individual goals and addresses multiple learning styles. Learning takes place in non-threatening and non-judgmental authentic environments, unlike the traditional classroom or workplace. A course like this is ideal for institutions wishing to incorporate the principles of the learner-centered college (Wilson et al., 2000).

Students report a multitude of benefits associated with service-learning courses, including enriched learning, skill development, increased self-esteem, job contacts, enhanced critical thinking skills, increased civic literacy, and an appreciation of diversity both in the classroom setting and at the service site (Brevard Community College, 2006). An additional benefit for students is that the community experience is documented on their academic transcripts. Stand-alone service-learning courses can magnify many of these benefits by focusing readings, discussions, and other class work on topics that relate directly to these areas.

Literature that is appropriate for stand-alone service-learning courses can be found in multiple disciplines, including education, psychology, political science, history, and sociology, among others. Any materials that address such issues as citizenship, community, the importance of education and free speech in a democratic society, universal human obligations, social justice, and social change are relevant. Beyond behavioral and social sciences, students can relate many concepts from these courses to other disciplines as well as to their personal growth.

This chapter outlines four models for stand-alone service-learning options, drawn from actual courses taught at Brevard Community College:

- Community Involvement (SOW 2054)

- Honors Community Involvement (SOWH 2054)

- Human Service Experience I, II, and III (SOW 1051-1053)

- Service-Learning Field Studies I (SOW 2948)

Community Involvement (SOW 2054)

Basic Requirements:

- Completed service-learning contract

- 32 documented hours at an approved project or service site

- 24 hours of seminar class work

- 3,000-word writing requirement (per the state of Florida)

Course Objectives:

> To develop a personal understanding of service and citizenship in many different facets of our diverse community through both practice and critical reflection.

Community Involvement was initially offered in 1991 and became a social science core course in 1996. This three-credit-hour course is designed to fit a 16-week semester. The instructor has some flexibility with respect to the class calendar. Traditionally, the class has been scheduled to meet every other week for three consecutive hours, allowing time when the class does not meet to complete community service hours. This frees some time for our constrained student population. However, the course can be scheduled to meet once a week or on a different schedule.

The course is student-driven; students choose the community project or site based on their own preferences. What they gain from their personal experience is related to themes that the class explores as a group. Depending on the scope of the service-learning program, students may be able to choose from hundreds of diverse agencies and organizations. Even though the students have very different experiences at their sites, the instructor is able build on themes that are common to all experiences, such as civic engagement, personal responsibility, and leadership. The course is organized around these themes through selected readings, activities, and extensive shared class discussion, but the students provide the substance of the course.

Major topics include the following (see Appendix 3A at the end of this chapter for a complete description of the course objectives and plan):

- Introduction to service-learning
- Citizenship skills within a democratic community and valuing diversity
- Critical reflection methodology and tenets of good performance
- Assessing the needs of a diverse community and the role of effective communication
- Service outside the student's own social, economic, racial, and cultural background
- Leadership and community service-learning

Individual faculty members can generate their own reading list for these themes, but an excellent starting point is Gail Albert's *Service-Learning Reader: Reflections and Perspectives on Service* (1994). Albert's reader is a compendium of short stories, essays, speeches, and parables that not only address the themes of a community service course head on, but also challenge assumptions and provoke thought.

Another good source is *Service-Learning: A Guide for College Students* (1989), published by ACTION/National Center for Service Learning. Campus Compact's widely used *Introduction to Service-Learning Toolkit* (2003) offers dozens of readings for faculty, most of which are equally appropriate for students. Campus Compact also offers an annotated reference list, *Essential Resources for Campus-based Service, Service-Learning, and Civic Engagement* (2004). (Both of these publications are available through the organization's website at www.compact.org/publications.) At Brevard, we also commonly use a booklet of handouts and readings compiled by the college's Community Involvement instructors. If your institution does not have such a resource, you may consider putting a team together to create one.

Extensive, focused reflection activities are an important part of Community Involvement students' ability to harvest and learn from their experiences. Frequently students are asked to form communities within the class and do assignments together, such as debate issues and write papers, glean meaning from readings, answer specific debriefing questions, or cooperatively define terms such as community, citizenship, engagement, charity, and social change. Students may even take group exams. In other words, students study community by being part of a community.

Another unique aspect of the course is that it is actually applied social science. Since social science is interdisciplinary and encompasses political science and the societal and geopolitical impact of environmental and other issues, work in the community relates to social science even when the work itself is in a different field. Students entering this course should expect to have experiences that may fall outside of their comfort zone and that will certainly differ substantially from what takes place in most college classrooms. The setting is dynamic rather than static, exposing students to new people, places, emotions, insights, and conflicts that may challenge their core belief system and values. In courses like this, faculty members may find themselves more than usually challenged to handle unique student issues, including emotional issues.

Students taking Community Involvement receive three credit hours in social and behavioral science and fulfill a general education requirement. Given its multidisciplinary nature, faculty members from a number of different academic fields can be credentialed to teach this course, including those in social work, psychology, education, public administration, social science, sociology, communications, English, human services, counseling, criminal justice, humanities, or health sciences.

Honors Community Involvement (SOWH 2054)

Basic Requirements:

- Admission into Honors Program
- Completed service-learning contract
- 32 documented hours at an approved community project or service site
- 3,000-word writing requirement (per the state of Florida)

Course Objectives:

> To develop a personal understanding of service, citizenship, leadership, and cultural diversity through critical reflection and action. Honors students will be guided in developing a commitment to full participation in the life of their communities and in determining their leadership roles in the community. The course will offer an interdisciplinary approach in putting theories into practice.

Honors Community Involvement is a relatively new course that has been offered since fall 2002. This three-credit-hour course is designed to fit a 16-week semester. The instructor has some flexibility with respect to the class calendar, although the structure of the honors class demands more continuity, communication, and instructor contact than does the regular Community Involvement course. Faculty have found that the most effective schedule is to meet with the class on a weekly basis for an hour and a half.

One difference between the regular and honors Community Involvement courses is that students enrolled in the regular course have more freedom in their selection of a service site or project. Students enrolled in the honors course are more limited in their site selection because of the format of the course. Another key difference is that the honors course requires a much greater commitment to teamwork than do regular classes. This course is a unique experience for students and faculty members alike.

Honors classes are typically small and the students highly motivated, offering a perfect opportunity to shift the locus of control from the faculty member to the students. The method of instruction for this class is flexible yet meaningful, experientially rich, and assessable for grading purposes. The syllabus for Honors Community Involvement (see Appendix 3B) serves as a generic "road map" for the course—one that can take many paths, detours, and pit stops if necessary, while still leading students to destinations both expected and unexpected.

The syllabus reflects specific assignments involving a journal, an interview, a survey, and a final examination that can be applied to any social problem. What it does *not* reflect is a class topic, text, readings, guest speakers, field trip destinations, a calendar of assignment due dates, or the specific format of the final exam. These aspects of the course aren't on the syllabus because the class makes these decisions as a group after the term begins, with the faculty member serving as a resource for transportation, clerical support, administrative and community contact, readings, and other assorted duties associated with the topic or demands of the class.

Planning and Placement (weeks 1–4)

Faculty members have found that it is best to start the first day by making introductions and explaining the class's basic requirements, objectives, and structure, since some students are uncomfortable in a course that relies heavily on team decision making and evolving assignments and goals. Honors Community Involvement also requires students to work at a site that supports the theme the class chooses. For example, if the class decides to focus on literacy, students must do their service at agencies whose work relates to this topic. Class members do not have to join the same agency, but everyone's service site should reinforce the theme under study. Emphasizing these aspects of the course at the outset gives students who have conflicting commitments the option of enrolling in non-honors Community Involvement if it better serves their needs or interests.

The first day of class is also the time to generate discussion about the social problem or issue that students would like to focus on for the semester. The class can spend some time brainstorming different class topics or projects. It is especially helpful if the faculty member has access to a directory of local agencies. For example, the Brevard Community College Center for Service-Learning has a directory called The Link that lists more than 300 social agencies in the county (see www.brevard.cc.fl.us/csl/content/link.html). This type of resource can be used to help facilitate class discussion.

Once the topic has been chosen, the class should spend the next three to four weeks addressing other key aspects of the course, including placement, calendar, text/readings, and community resources.

Placement. Students should get placed at an appropriate service site as quickly as possible. If your institution has a center for service-learning, it can facilitate this process. If not, students and faculty members will need to work together to generate a list of agencies and contacts. It helps for faculty members to have a core list of agencies from which to start.

Calendar. It's useful to generate a calendar of class dates for the students to help keep everyone focused on what goals need to be accomplished throughout the course. Due dates and timelines for assignments can take student input into account. Try to allow for some flexibility in the scheduling of assignments and projects as the course evolves. A good way to keep students on track is to develop a class agenda for each week the course meets. One of the students can take the minutes of each class.

Text/Readings. Search for current stories, articles, and readings that can enhance the class topic. Assistance in generating these materials can come from the college's media specialist, colleagues, or even the students. Readings from Albert's *Service-Learning Reader* (1994) or similar sources are also useful as they reinforce many of the underlying principles of service in a multidisciplinary fashion. Assignments from these readings can be tailored to fit the class's instructional needs.

Community Resources. Once students have selected a social issue, try to identify potential guest speakers from local agencies that work to address that need. It is a good idea to line up guest speakers for the fourth and fifth week of class if possible to give students an early opportunity to talk to local experts about the choson topic. Asking students to develop questions for the speaker prior to his or her arrival will help ensure a thoughtful discussion.

Fieldtrips to various agencies or facilities also serve as excellent enrichment activities and provide opportunities for the class to bond as a group. For example, if the class topic centers on recycling, an excursion can be planned during class time to visit the county landfill. If the topic involves crime or the legal system, it is appropriate to take the class on a tour of the county jail.

Again, a service-learning center can be a wonderful resource for locating community experts because of its established links between the college and the community. Representatives from the center and from community organizations are usually delighted to talk with students about their programs and service projects. Service-learning, and particularly this course, offers a win-win situation for everyone involved.

Goal Setting (weeks 5–6)

By the fifth week of the term, preliminary planning is out of the way and the class has had time to get acquainted and become comfortable with the course theme. Students should also have had sufficient time to get placed and spend some time working at their respective service sites. It is time to explore different projects that can serve as potential final examinations.

In this course, the final examination assessment is limited only by the imagination of the faculty member and the class. At Brevard, every attempt is made to make the exam as relevant and meaningful as possible. For example, one honors class spent a semester investigating recycling efforts within Brevard County. After much brainstorming, the class came up with the idea of developing a puppet show for preschool children that focused on environmental awareness and how children can do their part to save resources and not pollute. (See Appendix 3C for the instructions and grading matrix for this final project.) The class used recyclable products such as socks and egg cartons to make the puppets. They wrote a script appropriate for children ages 3–5 that incorporated information about recycling and then presented it to preschool children at the college's childcare center.

This final project reflected several key themes of the course. Presenting recycling information for young children helped students distill the knowledge they had acquired. It also reinforced the service orientation of the class. Finally, it got students to think in creative ways about how to reuse as well as recycle materials. The show was a huge success: it was hard to tell who was more enthusiastic and excited about the program, the honors students or the preschool kids.

Another final examination project involved the topic of domestic abuse. Students were to prepare a booth for an upcoming Women's History Day expo. The expo is an opportunity for social agencies that serve the needs of women to advertise their programs to students and the community at large. Each honors student was responsible for promoting his or her service site at the expo. Preparation for and participation in the expo were calculated as part of the final grade. In their preparations, students were asked to develop brochures about their agency individually. The local Salvation Army Domestic Violence shelter was so impressed with its brochure that the agency formally adopted it for use (see Appendix 3D).

The possibilities for projects are endless. Students can draw from their service sites, their service-learning center, class guest speakers, personal connections, or personal experiences for ideas. Brainstorming during class works very well. Students may need reminding that the term lasts for only a certain number of weeks. Whatever their goal, it needs to be accomplished within that timeframe. Keep in mind that class time can be utilized for the project, allowing students the opportunity to bond, interact, brainstorm, troubleshoot, delegate, and organize.

Once the project has been formulated, you'll need to develop a rubric for assessing the project. As yourself, What service is being provided to the community? What needs are being met? What community resources are available to help the project and the students? What should students be learning from the experience academically, civically, and personally? A participation element should be included in the rubric.

Self and peer grading can be very effective in this kind of class as it relies so heavily on group dynamics.

Ideally, the final examination project takes place at the end of the term. However, being flexible with this standard can open the door to some exciting possibilities. For example, the Women's Expo described earlier took place in the middle of March. Although this isn't the typical time period for a final exam, the event gave the students an opportunity to showcase their work in a genuine public environment. Education doesn't get more real than this!

Other Assignments (weeks 7–16)

Once the topic of the course has been identified and the final examination project determined, the calendar can continue to evolve. Again, it is a good idea to have an updated weekly agenda for the class to keep everyone on track. Deadlines become more concrete as the term unfolds.

The remainder of the term should center on the group work associated with the completion of the final project, the integration of guest speakers into the curriculum, and the students' work at their respective sites. Additional relevant assignments can be generated as necessary. For example, students can be assigned to conduct research on a given topic and then report out to the group, or assignments can be built around readings suggested by students or the faculty member.

Typically, students turn in their journals on the last day of class. One concluding activity, which can be especially beneficial for both students and faculty members, is to have students fill out a questionnaire on their class experience. (See Appendix 3E for an example.) The questionnaire can be handed out the week prior to the last class and then serve as a springboard for discussion and reflection. This tool provides excellent feedback for the instructor and also provides documentation for the institution.

Helpful Hints for Those Honored to Teach Honors

Emphasize the Evolving Nature of the Class on Day One. Some students will be insecure about not knowing the format of their final exam or the nature of certain assignments when the class begins. To assuage these fears, go over the process for creating assignments and establish reasonable timelines for completion. Flexibility is key to success here, since most likely this will be a new experience for both you and your students. Recognize that some tasks may take longer than others and try to gauge accordingly; be prepared to alter deadlines in some cases. Identify the deadlines that are non-negotiable as early in the term as possible and communicate them to all class members. This keeps everyone on track.

Utilize Technology and Campus Resources. It is a good idea to have all members of the class swap telephone numbers and emails early on in the semester. This can save a lot of time and confusion, as students will rely heavily on each other throughout the term. Also, with the administration's permission, utilize the campus resources for community contacts, printing and computer needs, and technical support in implementing class projects.

Use Your Time Well. Some faculty members are not comfortable with the idea of using class time for students to work on class projects or assignments. Teamwork is a critical component of this course for the experiential development of leadership, initiative, and personal responsibility, as well as for the appreciation of the diverse skills and backgrounds others have to offer. Teamwork is a dynamic and important way to build enthusiasm for the project and goals of the class.

Given the time constraints of most community college students, it is necessary to use some class time for planning, coordinating, and discussing work. It can also be useful to set aside some class time for tasks like running errands or making phone calls. With community service projects, students recognize that their individual grades are not as important as getting the project completed since community members are actually depending on them. It is important to keep this in mind when feeling reluctant to utilize class time for these projects.

Don't Be Overwhelmed. In some ways, teaching a class like Honors Community Involvement is like taking on a new course each term, with new topics, new readings, and new projects. Don't be daunted by what looks like a lot of extra work. In some ways it is more work, yet in many ways it isn't. Each term the topic, activities, and students are new, but the logistics of coordinating, organizing, and facilitating remain the same. Ideally, once the course topic is chosen and the final examination determined, the students in essence run the class with the instructor acting as facilitator and participant.

When weighing whether the time investment to create such a course is worth it to you, bear in mind that what this course does for students it also does for the instructor. It encourages creativity, spontaneity, and self-discovery through active learning. It offers the opportunity to bond with highly motivated people both on campus and in the community, and to become familiar with their unique talents and abilities. Finally, it increases awareness of the community's resources, connections, and needs.

Human Service Experience I, II, and III (SOW 1051-1053)

Basic Requirements (for each course):

- Completed service-learning contract or plan
- A minimum of 20 documented hours at an approved site
- Completed journal, essay, or other reflection tool
- 4 hours of reflection seminars

Course Objectives:

> To learn through service experience(s) to derive academic, personal, civic, and occupational benefits from community work.

Human Service Experience I, II, III are one-credit elective courses that can be taken concurrently or individually. These "pure" service-learning courses offer students the perfect opportunity to be introduced to the benefits associated with service-learning without having to make a lengthy time commitment. Because the courses can be taken sequentially, they allow interested students to continue to explore their service site over time for additional academic credit and concomitant benefit, or to try something completely new (again for academic credit). Offering flexible service and learning options like this one is a cornerstone to the success of any service-learning program.

SOW 1051 Human Service Experience allows students to select from any approved service site they choose to fulfill the course requirements. As a class, it meets four times (for one-hour seminars) in a given term. The first seminar covers an introduction to service-learning, the requirements of the course, distribution of forms, and community partner possibilities. The remaining seminars are devoted to assisting students with any questions or concerns they have regarding their service experiences and written work, reflection activities, and debriefing questions to enhance their civic and academic learning. (See Appendix 3F for a sample syllabus.)

Appropriate readings on civic education and related topics enhance the learning experience and provide additional context for reflection. The final seminar is often devoted to students sharing short presentations about the personal meaning and value of their service experience. This sharing of experiences is generally the most meaningful and memorable of all the seminars. Both the students and the faculty member get a chance to hear about the diverse range of projects, agencies, problems, needs, tragedies, and success stories about their own community.

Service-Learning Field Studies I (SOW 2948)

Basic Requirements:

- Completed service-learning contract
- A minimum of 20 documented hours at an approved site
- Completed journal, essay, or other reflection tool
- Attendance at a late-semester reflection seminar

Course Objectives:

> Gain experience in a public/human service setting that enables students to learn practical applications of the concepts taught in the classroom.

Student Competencies:

- Explain and define service-learning

- Formulate measurable service-learning goals

- Demonstrate the interrelatedness of the service field component with regular course academic concepts and principles

- Explain the meaning and benefits of service-learning for self, service setting, and society

- List and complete the necessary service experience documentation forms

Service-Learning Field Studies is a popular, easy method to expose students and faculty to the many benefits associated with service-learning. Service-Learning Field Studies is offered as a fourth-credit option added to courses within specific disciplines. For instance, if students are taking Sociology SYG 2000, they may also sign up for SYG 2948, Sociology Service-Learning Field Studies. For this class they must perform at least 20 hours of community service at an acceptable site, complete a class product such as a journal, essay, or presentation, and attend a mid-semester reflection seminar. At the end of the term they receive a grade in the one-credit class just as they do for their other classes.

Brevard students may take this elective course up to three times, as long as it is taken in three separate disciplines. (The option has been approved in 35 subjects.) Only students enrolled in classes whose instructors have added this as an option to their regular three-credit classes may register for the course.

Benefits for faculty members of this type of course include the ability to reinforce and enrich course content, an opportunity to devise customized ways to teach classroom concepts and principles, better-motivated students, faculty-generated FTE for the department, and independent study pay per student enrolled. For students, benefits include an extra elective credit within a discipline, documented service hours on their transcript, enriched academic learning, the ability to explore a career/major, the ability to apply course concepts to aid the community, the establishment of community and job contacts, improved self-confidence, and the development of life, occupational, and civic skills.

At Brevard, the basic steps involved for faculty interested in developing a service-learning fourth-credit option include the following:

1. Determine if you wish to offer a fourth-credit option and then contact the Center for Service-Learning to discuss placement options, procedures, forms, responsibilities, and deadlines.

2. The Center for Service-Learning will input the course into the system and add it to the list of fourth-credit options.

3. Peruse the provided sample Service-Learning Field Studies I course plan (see Appendix 3G) and promulgate a syllabus.

4. Specify appropriate service sites for your discipline; use the Center for Service-Learning directory or your own list.

5. Announce the option in your classes and/or have a speaker from the Center come to the classroom to explain it.

6. Refer students to the Center for Service-Learning for registration, service placement, appropriate documentation forms, and a service-learning contract.

7. Complete section 2 of the Fourth-Credit-Option Service-Learning Contract specifying assignments or requirements for the course (see Appendix 3H).

8. Facilitate or refer students to a mandatory student reflection seminar arranged by the Center for Service-Learning. Students are required to meet only once; however, you can arrange more reflection meetings.

9. Ensure integration of the service experience with course content—that is, tie in your own course objectives and suggestions in assigning journals or essays.

10. Scrutinize and grade requisite reflection methods for your class: journal, essay, summary, oral presentation, etc.

11. Have students complete a service-learning questionnaire.

12. Assign a grade.

The information above, along with sample syllabi, seminar schedules, reflection tools, information for students, and the forms shown in Chapter 2 of this book (e.g., the Placement Confirmation and Hour Report forms) are collected in a Fourth-Credit Guide for Faculty produced by the Center for Service-Learning. If you or other colleagues develop your own materials, it can be useful to combine them in one place to give students and faculty members a central resource.

Reflection Seminars

As noted earlier, students taking Service-Learning Field Studies must attend a mid-semester reflection seminar scheduled by the Center for Service-Learning. Students can choose from several seminars scheduled in November or April. The one-hour seminar brings together students from different disciplinary backgrounds to share written and oral reflection. Faculty members from a variety of disciplines are eligible to facilitate the session.

The Center for Service-Learning provides the facilitator with written reflection seminar debriefing questions (see Appendix 3I), which are applicable to all students regardless of their individual academic backgrounds or service experiences. The forms with these questions pass through several sets of hands. Each student receives a copy to use as a guide for discussion then returns it to the facilitating instructor, who writes comments about each student's participation in the seminar. The forms then go to the Center for Service-Learning to document students' participation before being sent on to the students' individual faculty members. This process ensures communication and documentation among all parties involved in the grading process.

Helpful Hints

Following are some additional tips for using a fourth-credit option:

- Outline all requirements and expectations in the syllabus and present the option at the start of the semester to give students ample time to take advantage of the program. Advertise and promote it. If appropriate, ask representatives from your service-learning center to speak to your classes about it.

- Identify what you want your students to get out of the experience. For example, if you are teaching an education course and you allow students to volunteer at day care centers, specify the kinds of behavior, interactions, and relationships you want your students to observe. Tailor your reflection assignment accordingly.

- Emphasize that you must approve the service site selection; otherwise be prepared for unusual student interpretations of what constitutes an "appropriate" site. Without guidance, students have been known to "serve" at for-profit companies whose work is entirely unrelated to their discipline.

- Although the course should have a minimum service requirement, be sure that students know that they can do more than the minimum number of hours.

- Set a realistic deadline for enrollment in the fourth-credit option. At Brevard, the deadline is usually by the sixth or seventh week of class.

- Make sure the syllabus includes the deadlines for students to get placement confirmation and a service-learning contract to you.

- Remember that students receive a separate grade for this elective; it is possible that this grade will differ from their regular course grade.

If you choose any of these stand-alone service-learning options, be prepared to approach the course with clear goals and an open mind. You may be surprised by what you learn as well as by what you're able to teach.

References

ACTION/National Center for Service-Learning. (1989). *Service-learning: A guide for college students.* Washington, DC: ACTION/NCSL.

Albert, G. (Ed.). (1994). *Service-learning reader: Reflections and perspectives on service.* Raleigh, NC: National Society for Experiential Education.

Brevard Community College, Center for Service-Learning. (2006). *Student volunteer/service-learning questionnaire results, fall 2005 – spring 2006.* Unpublished.

Campus Compact. (2003). *Introduction to service-learning toolkit: Readings and resources for faculty* (2nd ed.). Providence, RI: Campus Compact.

Campus Compact. (2004). *Essential resources for campus-based service, service-learning, and civic engagement.* Providence, RI: Campus Compact.

Heffernan, K. (2001). *Fundamentals of service-learning course construction.* Providence, RI: Campus Compact.

Wilson, C.D., Miles, C.L., Baker, R.L., & Schoenberger, R.L. (2000). *Learning outcomes for the 21st century: Report of a community college study.* Phoenix, AZ: League for Innovation in the Community College.

Appendix 3A

Community Involvement: Course Objectives and Plan

SIGNATURES

Curriculum Coordinator_____ Date _____

Curriculum Chair_____ Date _____

COURSE TITLE

Community Involvement

PREREQUISITE

Appropriate reading and writing scores on the entry-level placement test.

COREQUISITE	LAB FEE
None	None

COLLEGE-CREDIT HOURS: 03	VOCATIONAL-CREDIT HOURS: 00	CONTACT HOURS (PER TERM): 24

COURSE DESCRIPTION

Provides the student with a unique opportunity to examine community service and citizenship in many different facets of our diverse community through both practice and critical reflection. This is a designated diversity infused course.

COURSE OBJECTIVE(S)

Each student will be able to develop a personal understanding of service and citizenship and an increased awareness of cultural diversity through critical reflection and action; to develop a commitment to full participation in the varied lives of their communities; and to use an interdisciplinary approach to put theories into practice.

ACCELERATION MECHANISM(S) (METHOD(S) OF VALIDATING PRIOR LEARNING)

None

MAJOR TOPICS	STUDENT CLOCK HOURS	
	LECTURE	LAB
A. Introduction to service-learning	2	0
B. Citizenship skills within a democratic community and valuing diversity	3	0
C. Critical reflection methodology and tenets of good performance	1	0
D. Assessing the needs of a diverse community and the role of effective communication	1	0
E. Issues in service and volunteerism	3	0
F. Service outside the student's own social, economic, racial, and cultural background	2	0
G. To serve or not to serve	3	0
H. Leadership and community service-learning	3	0
I. Opportunities for community involvement and citizenship	3	0
J. Integration of the experience with the rest of life	3	0
K. The learning experience	0	32
	24	32

STUDENT COMPETENCIES, SKILLS, KNOWLEGE RELATIVE TO MAJOR TOPICS	EVALUATION METHODOLOGY
A. The student will delineate the forms, functions, roles, principles, benefits, history, and theoretical frameworks of community service-learning	Completion and quality of planning and reflective written instruments
B. The student will demonstrate a critical understanding of community, democracy and citizenship, and cultural diversity	Class participation
C. The student will demonstrate competency in utilizing critical reflection self-learning skills and the ability to communicate to persons of various ethnic backgrounds and cultures	Oral presentation, class participation

D. The student will participate in a service-learning opportunity that will expand awareness of community diversity

Project essay and evaluations

E. The student will describe the benefits and limits of community service

Written or oral presentation

F. The student will discuss the reasons for and against mandatory service

Written or oral presentation

G. The student will learn the skills necessary for effective leadership in diverse community service settings

Documentation of service project

H. The student will describe the impact of the service-learning experience on his/her life

Written or oral presentation

I. The student will estimate attainment of service and learning objectives/outcomes achievement

Oral and written assignments and documentation of service performance

Appendix 3B

Honors Community Involvement: Course Objectives and Plan

SIGNATURES

Curriculum Coordinator_____ Date_____

Curriculum Chair_____ Date_____

COURSE TITLE

Honors Community Involvement

PREREQUISITE

Admission into Honors Program

COREQUISITE	LAB FEE
None	None

COLLEGE-CREDIT HOURS: 03	VOCATIONAL-CREDIT HOURS: 00	CONTACT HOURS (PER TERM): 24

COURSE DESCRIPTION

Provides the Honors Program student with a unique opportunity to examine community service, citizenship, and leadership through both practice and critical reflection. Completion of this course will satisfy the community service requirement for those seeking an Honors Program diploma.

COURSE OBJECTIVE(S)

Each student will be able to develop a personal understanding of service, citizenship, leadership, and cultural diversity through critical reflection and action. Honors students will be guided to develop a commitment to full participation in the life of their communities and in determining their leadership roles in the community. The course will offer an interdisciplinary approach in putting theories into practice.

ACCELERATION MECHANISM(S) (METHOD(S) OF VALIDATING PRIOR LEARNING)

Instructor evaluation

MAJOR TOPICS	STUDENT CLOCK HOURS	
	LECTURE	LAB
A. Introduction to service-learning	3	0
B. Assessing and researching community assets/needs	3	0
C. Developing, implementing, and evaluating community projects	3	0
D. Issues in service and community diversity	3	0
E. Information gathering and research methods	3	0
F. Leading a community service project	3	0
G. Opportunities for community involvement and citizenship	3	0
H. Integration of the experience with the rest of life	3	0
I. The community service project	0	32
	24	32

STUDENT COMPETENCIES, SKILLS, KNOWLEGE RELATIVE TO MAJOR TOPICS	EVALUATION METHODOLOGY
A. The student will delineate the forms, functions, roles principles, benefits, history, and theoretical frameworks of community service-learning	Completion and quality of planning and reflective written instruments
B. The student will demonstrate a critical understanding of community mapping of assets and needs	Class participation
C. The student will demonstrate competency in developing and completing a community project	Oral presentations
D. The student will demonstrate an increased awareness of community diversity and service issues	Project essay and evaluations
E. The student will learn techniques to gather information through observation, recording, and communication skills	Documentation of service project
F. The student will learn the skills necessary for effective leadership of a community service project	Documention of service project
G. The student will describe the opportunities for and obstacles to community involvement and responsibility	Oral or written presentation

H.	The student will describe the impact of the service-learning project on his/her life	Oral or written presentation
I.	The student will estimate attainment of service and learning objectives/outcomes achievement	Oral and written assignments, documentation of service project

Appendix 3C

Honors Community Involvement: Sample Final Examination

INSTRUCTIONS

1. Prepare a puppet show illustrating the importance of recycling suitable for small children.

2. Puppets, props, and stage equipment should be constructed out of recyclable materials such as socks, egg cartons, soda cans, etc. Use your imagination.

3. Time limit should be 15–20 minutes; kids have short attention spans.

4. Factual information about recycling should be incorporated into show—make sure that it is age appropriate.

5. Handouts, literature, or favors should be provided for kids.

6. The show can include one or more vignettes.

GRADING

Areas that will be graded include the following:

1. Factual information incorporated. (Each participant should provide at least one source of documented information, a copy of which will be provided to the instructor at the time of the show.)

2. Time requirement met.

3. Use of recyclable products/creativity/imagination.

4. Division of labor. All members of group will be responsible for having a speaking role in the show. However, I am aware much work may be associated with what goes on behind the scenes. For example:

   a.   Script writing

   b.   Construction of puppets

   c.   Set/prop construction

   d.   Rehearsal/effort

I also realize that there are disadvantages associated with group work—e.g., some people shoulder more responsibility than do others. In an effort to be fair and to avoid conflict and excuses, your grade on this portion of the presentation will be assessed through self and peer grading. In other words, you will assign yourself a grade for the quality of your work and efforts in each of the above areas. You will also assign your fellow classmates a grade using the same criteria. The points you receive will be determined according to the average of the points generated through this method. A breakdown of how the calculations will be made follows.

Evaluation Matrix

AREA	WORTH (PTS)
1. Factual information incorporated	10
2. Time requirement met	5
3. Use of recyclable products/creativity/imagination	15
4. Division of labor	60
5. Other	10
TOTAL	100 points

Appendix 3D

Brochure Created for Honors Community Involvement Final Project

SERVICES TO VICTIMS OF DOMESTIC VIOLENCE

24–Hour Domestic Violence Hotline provides access to information, referrals, and assistance with safety and escape planning for victims of domestic violence and their families. The hotline also serves as the after-hours injunction for protection forwarding service for the Clerk of Court.

Confidential Emergency Shelter is a safe place for victims of domestic violence and their children to escape the abuse and improve their lives through counseling, accessing resources, and living in an emotionally supportive environment.

Domestic Violence Support Group for adult victims of domestic violence is a healing environment dedicated to lending emotional support, education about domestic violence dynamics, and assistance with safety planning.

Parenting Education Support Group provides parents and caregivers with tools and knowledge to cope with the stress of child-rearing and the effects of domestic violence on children.

Employability Skills Training Group improves the knowledge and skills of victims of domestic violence to become self sufficient and independent from the abuser through learning resume writing, job searching, and interviewing.

Children's Domestic Violence Support Group gives children who have witnessed domestic violence or have experienced abuse directly a safe place to express feelings and learn healthy ways to cope with anger, shame, guilt, and fear.

Victims Advocacy empowers victims with resources to improve their situations through securing funds to relocate, recouping medical bills related to the crime, and moving through the complicated criminal and civil justice systems.

Emergency Cell Phone Project enables victims of domestic violence to call law enforcement in an emergency through use of cellular telephones at no cost.

Nurturing Parent Education Program provides families involved with dependency issues an intensive fifteen week parenting program in conjunction with supervised visitation at rotating sites (Cocoa and Palm Bay).

ALWAYS REMEMBER

You have the right to feel safe in your relationship. You are not alone. There are several agencies that can help.

Victim Advocacy,
Relocation, Assistance,
and Emergency
Cell Phone Project
(321) 631-2766 ext:16

The Salvation Army
Brevard County
Domestic Violence Program

P.O. Box 1540 Cocoa, FL 32923

Hotline: (321) 631-2764
Office: (321) 631-2766
Fax:(321) 631-7914

THE FAMILY ENRICHMENT CENTER

The Family Enrichment Center provides children the opportunity to visit with their non-custodial parent safely. Any issues relating to contact between non-custodial parents and their children are addressed and monitored; concerns ranging from children observing domestic violence to child abuse or neglect, to sexual molestation are understood and addressed by Center staff.

- Families are referred to the Center by either the Florida Department of Children and Family Services, or through a judicial or court system.

- **Supervised Visitation** allows contact between children and parents within a safe and structured environment in the presence of trained personnel.

- **Monitored Exchange** facilitates the safe transfer of children from one parent to the other for unsupervised visits by the non-custodial parent for the weekend, day, or evening visits.

- Our visits and exchanges occur at either our site in Cocoa or our site in Palm Bay, and specific arrangements are made to accommodate individual needs.

- In the initial intake interview for participation in the program, parties receive: arrival and departure appointments, fee schedules, visitation or exchange policies, and participation guidelines. Support services, information and referrals are offered as requested or required. All intakes are completed individually, and are required by all participants.

Appendix 3E

16 Questions/Many Answers:
A Service-Learning Debriefing Exercise

1. Describe what you learned and felt during your service project in two minutes or in two sentences.

2. Give two "feeling" words that exemplify your service-learning experience.

3. Draw a picture that conveys your experience.

4. What was the worst or most difficult thing that happened to you? (Tell what you learned about the experience.)

5. What was the best thing that happened? (Tell what you learned from that experience.)

6. Rate yourself from 1 to 10 for your performance. Why?

7. How have you benefited from your service-learning experience personally, academically, civically, and occupationally?

8. What have you learned about yourself from your service-learning experience?

9. What changes would you recommend in how your service site operates? How the service-learning program operates?

10. Name five things that you can do to better society.

11. How does your service experience relate to your academic work or courses?

12. Select a person you admired during your service-learning experience. Explain what you found admirable about this person.

13. Because of my service-learning experience, I am... (Complete this sentence.)

14. Compare or contrast your service-learning experience with anything you've previously experienced, read about, or imagined.

15. The college is proposing to require all students to do a 20-hour service-learning experience. Please list the pros and cons for this proposal from both a student perspective and a community agency perspective.

16. Add your own question(s).

Appendix 3F

Human Service Experience (SOW 1051, 1052, 1053): Sample Course Syllabus

This course offers an opportunity to gain service-learning experience in a public/human service organization. Through the interaction of experience and reflection, the student learns to apply knowledge and skills in the "real" world, exercises critical thinking, develops self-learning and helping skills, develops societal knowledge and sensitivity, and enhances personal development.

Learning Outcomes: Articulation of the meaning of service-learning and social responsibility, knowledge of human service settings and relationship to society, identification of skill competencies and needs, understanding of the relationship between theory and practice and concomitant benefits to the community, identification of ways to integrate service with life.

Seminar One: Class introduction, course/student expectations, service-learning discourse, placement possibilities, journal writing.

- Complete class registration and Service-Learning Application forms
- Receive documentation forms
- Receive Service-Learning Plan examples

Week 4/5 – No Formal Class Meeting: Placement/project site selected and confirmation form turned in to instructor by Friday of the 4th / 5th week of term.

- Submit Service-Learning Plan for instructor approval

Seminar Two: Discussion of service-learning experience and setting, relationship of theory and practice, levels of reflection, debriefing questions.

- Mid-term performance evaluations due; review journal and other written work

Seminar Three: Integration of experience with rest of life. Short presentation about the personal meaning and value of one's service.

- Complete Center for Service-Learning questionnaire
- Turn in written work
- Turn in final performance evaluation/service hour report
- Complete debriefing questions

EVALUATION CRITERIA	POINTS
Service experience: 20 service hours for each credit hour documented by hour report and performance evaluations	35
Seminars: Participation and attendance in all scheduled sessions (3); a final presentation about your service-learning experience	25
Written work: Completion and quality of service-learning plan, journal/final essay, and debriefing questions	40

Appendix 3G

Service-Learning Field Studies I: Sample Course Plan

SIGNATURES

Curriculum Coordinator_____ Date _____

Curriculum Chair_____ Date _____

FACULTY DISCIPLINE	FACULTY CREDENTIAL OPTION
Psychology	1

HONORS COURSE	REPEATABLE
No	No

SUITABLE FOR ONLINE	COURSE CREDITS	CLOCK HOURS	TYPE OF CREDIT
Yes	1	4	Elective

LAB FEE	SPECIAL COURSE FEE
None	None

PREREQUISITE	COREQUISITES
None	None

DEGREE TYPE

❏ A.A. ❏ A.A.S. ❏ A.T.D. ❏ A.S. ❏ C.C.C. (PSV) ❏ P.S.A.V.

TYPE

This course gives the student the opportunity to understand the relationship of theory to practice through participation in a service-learning experience. Students are required to complete 20 hours of service work, a service-learning contract, and necessary oral and written reflection methods.

PRIMARY COURSE OBJECTIVE(S)

Gain experience in a public/human service setting that enables students to learn practical applications of concepts taught in the classroom.

ACCELERATION MECHANISM(S) (METHOD(S) OF VALIDATING PRIOR LEARNING)

None

MAJOR TOPICS	STUDENT CLOCK HOURS	
	LECTURE	LAB
A. The concept of service-learning	0.5	0
B. Service-learning goals/plans	1.0	0
C. Synthesizing the field experience component and classroom learning	1.5	0
D. The meaning, benefits, and impacts of community involvement	1.0	0
E. The service-learning experience	0	20
	4.0	20

STUDENT COMPETENCIES, SKILLS, KNOWLEGE RELATIVE TO MAJOR TOPICS	EVALUATION METHODOLOGY
A. Explain and define service-learning functions, roles, principles, benefits, history, and theoretical frameworks	Completion and quality of planning and reflective methods
B. Formulate measurable service-learning goals	Completion and quality of planning and reflective methods
C. Demonstrate the interrelatedness of the service field component with academic concepts and principles (in psychology or other discipline)	Succeessful participation in mandatory reflection seminar
D. Explain the meaning and benefits of service-learning for self, service setting, and society	Documentation of the service-learning experience, including hour report and supervisor's performance evaluations of student
E. List and complete the necessary service experience documentation forms	

Appendix 3H

Service-Learning Contract: 4th Credit Field Study Option

SECTION I (Student Completes)	When Contract Section I, II, III are completed, give the white copy to instructor, yellow copy to the Service-Learning Office, and keep the pink copy for yourself.

Student Name:_____ Telephone #:_____ Student#:_____

STATE SERVICE AND LEARNING GOALS:

SERVICE: What exactly do you expect to do? Briefly describe the nature of the volunteer service work and why you have chosen it:

LEARNING: What do you expect to learn from this experience? (e.g. information and understanding about the elderly, people, environmental issues, teaching methods, etc.)

SKILLS: What skills do you expect to develop and learn from this experience? (e.g. communication skills, writing, problem solving, teaching techniques, etc.)

I agree to devote at least 20 hours this semester between the dates of _____ and _____ at (volunteer site/project) _____. I also agree to meet the academic or learning requirements that my professor has indicated in Section II in order to receive one hour of academic credit for this service-learning experience.

Student Signature: _____ Date: _____

SECTION II (Faculty Instructor Completes)	The student named above has my permission to engage in this 4th credit option service-learning experience to meet the requirement of _____ 2948. In addition to the 20 minimum of service hours required, the student will complete the following service-learning related assignments for the course.

REQUIREMENTS:

1. ❑ Journal   ❑ Oral Presentation   ❑ Final   ❑ Essay   ❑ Other _____

2. One midterm reflection seminar arranged by the Center for Service Learning is required. (See Section III)

3. Community Service-Learning Questionnaire must be completed at the end of the assignment.

4. Elaboration of evidence or academic work needed:

Faculty Member Signature: _____ Date: _____

SECTION III (Center for Service-Learning Completes)

❑ Registration Form Completed   ❑ Fees Paid   ❑ Service Documentation Forms Received

Course and Section: _____ Site Selection:_____

Midterm Seminar Selection: Campus: _____ Date: _____ Time:_____ Room: _____

The Service-Learning student has been given the necessary forms, has completed a registration form, confirmation form, and has scheduled a reflection seminar.

Service-Learning Staff Signature: _____Date:_____

Distribution: White (Faculty Member)   Yellow (CSL)   Pink (Student)

Appendix 31

Service-Learning Field Studies I:
Reflection Seminar Debriefing Questions

STUDENT NAME   DATE

4TH CREDIT INSTRUCTOR

---

1. What were your first impressions of the service site?

2. How was setting similar or different from what you expected?

3. Discuss your experience working with people of different backgrounds: economic status, ethnicity, race, religion, age, sexual orientation, physical ability, or health status. How has your perspective changed because of your service-learning experience?

4. What was most challenging or difficult? What did you learn from the experience?

5. What changes would you recommend in your service placement/project?

6. How have you benefited overall?

7. How does your service experience relate to your course or classroom work?

8. Has this service-learning experience changed your concept of civic responsibility and your desire to help others? How?

Seminar Facilitator Comments:

FACILITATOR SIGNATURE AND DATE

Assessing Service-Learning Outcomes

TANYA RENNER

$\mathscr{D}$OCUMENTING THE IMPACT OF SERVICE-LEARNING at any institution presents myriad challenges. Service-learning shifts education from the isolation and artificiality of the classroom to the real world, where many different kinds of learning may take place simultaneously. What students gain from their experiences is often rich, exciting, personally transforming, and beyond the reach of traditional pencil-and-paper tests (Eyler, 2000). In addition to the intricacy of assessing concurrent changes in learning on many different fronts, there are also both short-term and long-term changes, and assessment of the long-term changes has its own challenges.

Community colleges can play an important and unique role in researching learning outcomes, albeit with manifest limitations. This chapter summarizes the challenges and strengths that affect the ability of community colleges to assess service-learning outcomes, provides an example of one such research effort, and offers suggestions for strategies that community colleges can implement in order to make meaningful contributions to the research literature on learning outcomes for service-learning students.

Current Outcomes Assessment

Researchers have conducted a variety of learning outcome studies with service-learning students (see Eyler et al., 2001, for a summary of research through the 1990s). In addition to anticipated results of deeper exploration of course content, students report opportunities to apply their knowledge and to connect theory with practice (Renner & Hasager, 2004). Some have disclosed feeling a sense of empowerment regarding world issues, with a concomitant sense of civic responsibility (Sperling et al., 2003), while others have demonstrated critical thinking skills that transcend an individual course (Steinke & Buresh, 2002). In addition to immediate, and quite possibly short-term, learning, students may demonstrate lasting outcomes such as long-term retention of knowledge, changes in attitude toward civic responsibility, and behavioral commitment to the public good (see, for example, Koth, 2003; Raman & Pashupati, 2002; and Moely et al., 2002).

While many studies about such learning outcomes document that service-learning is a valuable teaching and learning strategy, exactly what students are learning, and how long this learning may endure, has not been definitively established (Eyler, 2000). Time-honored classroom assessment strategies that focus solely on course content do not reflect the wide array of learning outcomes possible with service-learning. Many of these potential results do not yet have recognized or widely used instruments for assessing them.

Application of rigorous scientific control to a learning strategy that is, by definition, beyond classroom control—and that results in myriad unexpected, and perhaps unacknowledged, learning outcomes—is complicated by the growing body of research indicating that participant characteristics are a critical mediating factor for the learning outcomes that may be observed (Sperling et al., 2003). To add to the intricacy of the issue, service-learning itself is not consistently defined, so part of the variability in research outcomes can be attributed to the nature and quality of the service-learning experience (Eyler & Giles, 1999).

In order to demonstrate that service-learning unequivocally enhances educational outcomes, one must show that the improvement in students' learning is directly connected to the service-learning experience. To do so would require a direct comparison of service-learning and non–service-learning students, with all other factors the same: students would need to be in the same class, with the same instructor, using the same instructional materials and methods. Even then, to eliminate any selection bias among students choosing to do service-learning, students would need to be randomly assigned to one group or the other. If the students in the service-learning section demonstrated greater learning at the end of the semester, the results would constitute scientific evidence that service-learning caused the students to learn more.

This type of comparison is difficult to make because it is usually not practical to randomly assign students to different conditions. For example, if the study is done within one classroom, students will see that others have different assignments and will wonder why they belong to a group that is treated differently. In addition, some of the experiences of the service-learning students will probably be reflected in class discussions, which means those randomly assigned not to participate in service-learning will still be exposed to some of the benefits of service-learning. If some sections of courses are randomly assigned to have service-learning while others do not, then many factors, such as time of day, day of the week, and perhaps even the instructor, will not be held constant and will likely contribute to measurement error.

Community Colleges and Service-Learning Assessment

Given the nature of traditional classroom learning assessment techniques and the laboratory control required to demonstrate cause and effect, it may seem that the complexity of measuring service-learning outcomes would pose unreasonable demands on the research capabilities of community colleges. Community colleges are primarily teaching, not research, institutions, and we serve broadly diverse student populations. Mundhenk (2004) points out several related challenges for community colleges attempting to do any kind of learning outcomes assessment:

- Open admissions policies result in student populations that vary from one semester to the next in terms of goals, abilities, resources, and so on.

- The typical community college infrastructure does not support faculty involvement in research, including assessment research.

- Primary responsibility for this type of research most often falls on an institutional research office that may be understaffed and have a variety of other priorities.

As Mundhenk (2004) summarizes, "Limited budgets and staff, a very transient student body, and institutional mission and values tend to make data-based assessment activities that involve extensive research more difficult, and consequently less pervasive, at community colleges" (p. 39).

Thus, issues that may impede community college assessment of service-learning outcomes include not only lack of established assessment strategies for service-learning and lack of agreement regarding the definition of many of the concepts (e.g., civic engagement) and the nature of the learning outcomes, but also the lack of ongoing, institutionally supported research into these issues.

Community colleges do, however, have other qualities and experiences that make them exceptionally well qualified to address some of the community-oriented issues in service-learning outcomes assessment. First, community colleges have deep and enduring relationships with external stakeholders and an ongoing, concomitant responsibility to deliver curricula that address community needs. (See Mundhenk, 2004; see also Prins, 2002, for a discussion of the potential for deepening constructive relationships between community partners and community colleges through service-learning.)

Second, as Ewell (2002, 2003) asserts, assessment of learning outcomes has meaning only in context—i.e., the value of learning for students vis-à-vis life beyond academia. To satisfy our shared mission, we must ensure that our students not only move successfully through our programs but also that they are able to take their learning with them when they move on to vocations or further education. Our relationships with community partners (including employers and other educational institutions where our students may transfer) require us to generate meaningful assessments, particularly in our vocational programs. This provides us with extensive experience in the kind of authentic learning outcomes assessment needed to evaluate service-learning outcomes (Mundhenk, 2004).

Community colleges that strive to assess service-learning outcomes may also find that they are simultaneously assessing results that are directly related to efforts to become more learner-centered. Recent investigations regarding effective education have generated a body of knowledge that delineates various principles for learning (Gollub et al., 2002, p. 119):

1. Structuring new and existing knowledge around a discipline's major concepts and principles facilitates learning with understanding.

2. Learners use what they already know to construct new understandings.

3. Learning is facilitated through the use of metacognitive strategies that identify, monitor, and regulate cognitive processes.

4. Learners have different strategies, approaches, patterns of abilities, and learning styles that are a function of the interaction between their heredity and their prior experiences.

5. Learners' motivation to learn and sense of self affect what and how much they learn, as well as how much effort they will put into the learning process.

6. The practices and activities in which people engage while learning shape what they learn.

7. Learning is enhanced through socially supported interactions.

There are striking similarities between these principles of learning and the kinds of experiences service-learning students may be expected to have:

- Service-learning supports different learning styles and abilities.

- Students may be required to use prior knowledge to construct understanding.

- Knowledge is constructed in a social context.

- Reflection activities promote metacognition.

- A variety of activities shape learning in different ways.

Thus, service-learning experiences may be seen as central to efforts to promote learner-centered education.

Community colleges that are actively participating in the paradigm shift to a more learner-centered mode of operation (see Barr & Tagg, 1995) need to develop ways of discovering what knowledge students are acquiring, and how, in order to improve efforts to bolster student learning. This is consistent with the requirements from accrediting agencies to develop a "culture of evidence" (Pacheco, 1999). In many cases, efforts to do so have resulted in the development of systems to monitor curriculum quality and learning outcomes.

When this monitoring is in turn integrated with ongoing efforts to respond to diverse student characteristics, needs, and goals, as well as to community and employment needs, the results can be powerful. In other words, the community college's long-standing relationships with a variety of external stakeholders place it in a unique position to accomplish authentic, meaningful learning outcomes assessment for service-learning as well as other kinds of interdisciplinary, learner-centered work.

One Campus's Approach:
A Case Study of Kapi'olani Community College

Kapi'olani Community College began its service-learning initiative in 1995. Since that time, nearly 6,000 service-learning students have contributed more than 150,000 hours of service to the community. Over the years, funding from the college's administration, the Corporation for National and Community Service, the Centers for Disease Control and Prevention, and the Kellogg Foundation—as well as recognition and support from organizations such as the Carnegie Foundation for the Advancement of Teaching, the Association of American Colleges and Universities, the American Council on Education, and Campus Compact—has contributed to the college's ability to institutionalize service-learning and to carry out high-quality innovation in programming.

Kapi'olani views service-learning as a teaching and learning method that integrates critical reflection and meaningful service in the community with academic learning, personal growth, and civic responsibility. Service-learning at the college encourages students and faculty to be active partners with community members in building stronger communities and provides students with opportunities to develop and demonstrate:

- Newly acquired knowledge, skills, and attitudes.

- Deeper understanding and application of course content and broader appreciation of the discipline.

- A deeper understanding of their relationship and responsibility to their local, national, regional, and global communities.

Service-learning at the college is designed specifically to support resilience and success for all students. It also supports a range of social/civic outcomes, such as healthy lifestyles, environmental sustainability, respect and care for the elderly, community safety, appreciation for diverse communities and cultures, and international collaboration.

Not long after the college's launch of the service-learning initiative, I implemented a quasi-experimental design at Kapi'olani to assess service-learning's effectiveness (Renner, 2003). Students who chose to do service-learning and students in the same classes who did not choose to do service-learning were all surveyed regarding their values and behaviors. Surveys were given at the beginning and at the end of the semester. This process was replicated three times over six years. Also analyzed were comparisons of GPA and retention rates for service-learners before and after service, and between service learners and non–service-learners.

These different kinds of evidence identified pre-existing differences between service-learners and non–service-learners: the service-learners tended to have higher GPAs, to be women, and to have done more community work already. After the service-learning experience, however, service-learners showed significantly greater differences both from their own pretest scores and from non–service-learners on several measures. After doing service-learning, students were more likely than ever to have a higher GPA than non–service-learners, more likely than ever to be volunteering more hours in the community, more likely to feel committed to being involved in the community, and more likely to respond positively to survey items that indicated a sense of connection ("My teachers care about me," "I try to talk to people who feel left out"). In addition, they were more likely to stay in school. Although the experimental design did not rule out the possibility that those students who chose to do service-learning would have experienced some differences anyway, it was concluded that those who chose service-learning profited from the experience.

More recent research into learning outcomes at Kapi'olani has addressed the ways that service-learning may enhance understanding of course content. Some of these assessment efforts have been limited to one campus, but several approaches have been part of statewide efforts to understand the value of service-learning across diverse educational and service experiences. For example, in conjunction with faculty and service-learning staff around the state, Hawai'i Pacific Islands Campus Compact (HIPICC—one of more than 30 state Campus Compact offices) developed a rubric to analyze student reflections that included dimensions for civic responsibility, critical thinking, and the ability to draw connections between practice and theory. Items on the rubric were informed not only by academic goals for service-learning but also by service-learning partners and employers in the community. This rubric has been used annually by Kapi'olani's service-learning student leaders to learn more about the strengths of various approaches to service-learning.

Another HIPICC program evaluation project utilized short essay responses from service-learning and non–service-learning students on the "three most important things you learned from this class." Kapi'olani was one participant in this statewide study, which showed that service-learners made more comments about what they had learned, expressed more community awareness and/or responsibility, and mentioned more applications of course content than did their non–service-learning counterparts (Renner et al., 2003; Renner & Hasager, 2004). Non–service-learners made more comments limited to course content, while there was no difference in number of comments regarding appreciation of course content.

A current project sponsored by HIPICC, Service-Learning and Critical Thinking (SeLeCT), involves four-year and community colleges from around the state, as well as community colleges in Guam and American Samoa. Faculty from around the Pacific are comparing service-learners' work with that of non–service-learners in the same courses on a variety of measures of critical thinking.

Both the college's assessment efforts and our assessment stakeholders are grounded in our communities. Campus and community members work together to assess outcomes across regions, disciplines, and types of educational institutions. To ensure adequate community input, we include community members in decision making, both formally (e.g., on our advisory boards) and informally.

Our service-learning model brings together many faculty, students, staff, and community members in learner-centered ways; so does the effort to continuously assess and adapt service-learning programs. Faculty come together across disciplines and institutions to generate common definitions and measures for important, but often abstract, learning outcomes such as quantitative reasoning, critical thinking, and written communication skill. We operate under the belief that assessment becomes authentic when it is done by community members providing needed services to real people; learning becomes authentic and learning communities are created when instructors, service-learners, and community members are all learning side by side; and integrity becomes a shared endeavor when all are involved in monitoring for quality assurance in service delivery as well as learning.

Looking Forward

Although the community college infrastructure poses important limitations, our expertise in community partnering and practical measures of learning are fundamental to understanding the impact of service-learning. We have a responsibility and an opportunity to contribute in a meaningful way to the research on this topic. How, then, can we maximize our resources and participate in the discovery of the depth and breadth of learning outcomes for service learners? Here are a number of suggestions, based on our experience at Kapio'lani Community College:

1. Collaborate with regional Campus Compact member institutions to develop profiles of service-learning for many different kinds of learning outcomes. Because Campus Compact's member institutions are dedicated to educating the next generation of civic leaders through service-learning and other forms of engagement, these institutions are a good place to start when seeking collaborators. (See www.compact.org/membership/by_location for a list of Campus Compact's 1,000+ member institutions by region.)

   • When we work with other community colleges, we increase our numbers and our resources.

- When we work with other four-year colleges and universities, we increase the diversity and potential applications for our work.

2. Work with community partners to develop evolving, practical (as well as abstract) definitions of intended learning outcomes such as critical thinking, workplace readiness, and civic engagement.

3. Hold workshops for faculty on how to connect service-learning efforts to the general education curriculum.

   - Ensure that faculty who teach full time are aware of and perhaps engaged in research efforts to document learning outcomes for service-learning.

   - Promote alignment of learning objectives on the syllabus for service-learning with general education standards.

   - Create interdisciplinary teams to develop appropriate measures for intended and desired learning outcomes such as quantitative reasoning, civic engagement, and communication skills.

4. Publish findings to help proliferate successful practices.

Through these types of collaborations, community colleges can take advantage of their unique community connections to advance the assessment—and thus the practice—of service-learning across institutions.

References

Barr, R., & Tagg, J. (1995). From teaching to learning: A new paradigm for undergraduate education. *Change, 27,* 12–25.

Ewell, P. (2002, June). *Perpetual movement: Assessment after twenty years.* Keynote address presented at the American Association for Higher Education Assessment Forum, Boston, MA. Retrieved August 20, 2007, from www.teaglefoundation.org/learning/pdf/2002_ewell.pdf.

Ewell, P. (2003). The learning curve. *BizEd, 2,* 28–33.

Eyler, J. (2000, Fall). What do we most need to know about the impact of service-learning on student learning? *Michigan Journal of Community Service-Learning,* Special Issue, 11–18.

Eyler, J., & Giles, D.E., Jr. (1999). *Where's the learning in service-learning?* San Francisco: Jossey-Bass.

Eyler, J., Giles, D.E., Stenson, C. & Gray, C. (2001). *At a glance: What we know about the effects of service-learning on college students, faculty, institutions and communities, 1993–2000* (third edition). Scotts Valley, CA: National Service-Learning Clearinghouse. Available at www.compact.org/resources/downloads/aag.pdf.

Gollub, J.P., Bertenthal, M.W., Labov, J.B., & Curtis, P.C. (Eds.). (2002). *Learning and understanding: Improving advanced study of mathematics and science in U.S. high schools.* Washington, DC: National Academy Press.

Koth, K. (2003). Deepening the commitment to serve: Spiritual reflection in service-learning. *About Campus, 7,* 2–7.

Moely, B.E., McFarland, M., Miron, D., Mercer, S., & Ilustre, V. (2002). Changes in college students' attitudes and intentions for civic involvement as a function of service-learning experiences. *Michigan Journal of Community Service-Learning, 9,* 18–26.

Mundhenk, R. (2004). Communities of assessment. *Change, 36,* 36–41.

Pacheco, D. (1999). A culture of evidence. *Assessment and Accountability Forum, 9.*

Prins, E. (2002). The relationship between institutional mission, service, and service-learning at community colleges in New York State. *Michigan Journal of Community Service-Learning, 8,* 35–39.

Raman, P., & Pashupati, K. (2002). Turning good citizens into even better ones: The impact of program characteristics and motivations on service-learning outcomes. *Journal of Nonprofit & Public Sector Marketing, 10,* 187–206.

Renner, T. (2003, November). *Converging data: Demonstrating service-learning effectiveness on our campus.* Paper presented at the Third Annual International Service-Learning Research Conference, Salt Lake City.

Renner, T., Davis, R., Hasager, U., & Pascua, A. (2003, April). *Assessing learning outcomes: Lessons brought to life by service-learning.* Paper presented at the Sixth Annual Continuums of Service Conference, Seattle.

Renner, T., & Hasager, U. (2004, March). *Service-learning and depth of understanding.* Paper presented at the Seventh Annual Continuums of Service Conference, San Diego.

Sperling, R., Wang, V., Kelly, J. & Hritsuk, B. (2003). Does one size fit all? The challenge of social cognitive development. *Michigan Journal of Community Service-Learning, 9,* 5–14.

Steinke, P., & Buresh, S. (2002). Cognitive outcomes of service-learning: Reviewing the past and glimpsing the future. *Michigan Journal of Community Service-learning 8,* 5–14.

Chapter Five

Service-Learning and the Scholarship of Teaching and Learning

DONNA KILLIAN DUFFY

> *I think the most important quote from the article on resiliency is "the ability to read at grade level by age ten is a startling predictor of resilience in poor and neglected children." I never understood the significance of this statement until I did community service at [a local] school.... While working in the classroom, I observed that the two students who misbehaved the most were the ones who had the most difficulty reading. If they are sent out of the room or to the office, they are now missing even more work. The amount of time spent on disciplining these kids is greater than the amount of time spent on individual reading programs.*
>
> *—Student Reflection*

WHAT CAN WE INFER ABOUT LEARNING from this student's reflection? We know that the student tried to connect a general statement about reading levels to two individuals in a classroom setting. We know that she grappled with the complex reality of balancing discipline, reading tutoring, and order in a typical classroom.

From a service-learning perspective, the student's quote suggests that the placement helped her to learn the content of the course, provided some skill in tutoring, and initiated questioning about issues of literacy, social inequalities, and behavior problems. In many respects, the student's analysis fits the suggestion of Huba and Freed (2000) that "an exemplary assessment task is one that involves college students in addressing enduring and emerging issues and problems that are ill-defined and of current relevance in their disciplines" (p. 224).

What can we learn about teaching practice by reflecting on this student's response? Students engaged in service-learning gain insight into their experiences through reflection; in a similar way, faculty engaged in the scholarship of teaching and learning gain insight into their practice by analyzing and reflecting on student work. The scholarship of teaching and learning (SoTL—pronounced soh-tul) generally begins with questions about student learning and requires systematic inquiry to answer these questions.

SoTL also involves peer review and results in products that can be shared with others. Lee Shulman (1998) suggests that for an activity to be designated as scholarship, it should manifest at least three key characteristics: it should be public, susceptible to critical review and evaluation, and accessible for exchange and use by other members of one's scholarly community. These characteristics apply to the four types of scholarship suggested by Ernest Boyer in *Scholarship Reconsidered* (1990): discovery, integration, application, and teaching. Translating them into classroom practice is the focus of the scholarship of teaching and learning.

SoTL can assist service-learning practitioners as they strive to deepen their craft. Both SoTL and service-learning aim to create a more "permeable" classroom—a place where "knowledge generated within it is extended beyond its boundaries" and into which "outside knowledge is assimilated" (Sandy, 1998). Service-learning accomplishes this by bringing experiences from the community to the classroom and information from the course back to the community. SoTL creates permeability by making student learning as accessible as possible by presenting it to others and by connecting broader theoretical perspectives to unique classroom experiences (see Figure 1).

Service-Learning as a Route to SoTL

According to Hutchings and Shulman (1999),

> The scholarship of teaching and learning is not synonymous with excellent teaching. It requires a kind of 'going meta' in which faculty frame and systematically investigate questions related to student learning—the conditions under which it occurs, what it looks like, how to deepen it, and so forth—and do so with an eye to not only improving their own classroom but to advancing practice beyond it. (p. 15)

The process of implementing service-learning provides an excellent setting for "going meta." Faculty typically use service-learning tentatively at first, but in time the practice expands to other courses and evolves in multiple new ways. How practice evolves into different pathways may provide important insights about ways to sustain service-learning work.

Faculty typically do not document this evolution, but doing so may help them to develop a deeper understanding of student learning. As Kozma (1985) states, "a clear line of ancestry can frequently be traced to the instructor's early experiences with the same or similar innovations that are broadened, extended, or mutated with subsequent generations" (p. 307). Documenting an experience with service-learning and then designing a SoTL project to address ongoing questions would not only assist faculty in their classroom but also "advance practice beyond it."

Shulman (1998), acknowledging the tension between conducting research studies and teaching in a classroom, questions, "What can one ask about a course in order to understand the ways in which its creation and conduct constitute a coordinated act of scholarship?" (p. 7). He suggests that teaching, like other forms of scholarship, is an extended process that unfolds over time involving at least five elements:

- Vision
- Design
- Interactions
- Outcomes
- Analysis

FIGURE 1:
The Permeable Classroom:
How Service-Learning and the Scholarship of Teaching and Learning (SoTL) Contribute to Knowledge Exchange

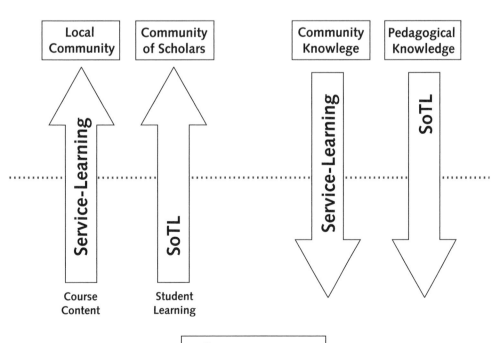

Making some or all of these elements public and open to review by peers is a critical part of the scholarship of teaching.

In 1998 I revised my Abnormal Psychology course around the generative topic of resilience, considered ways to integrate service-learning experiences in more deliberate ways in the classroom, and analyzed the work as a SoTL project (Duffy, 2000, available at www.middlesex.mass.edu/carnegie/MCCCG/Duffy_opening_lines.pdf). I explored a question in depth, had course materials reviewed by others, and made results public in presentations and publications (Duffy, 2004). This experience proved to be useful background for exploring other projects that link service-learning and SoTL.

Service-Learning Course Design as a SoTL Opportunity

A SoTL project begins with questions about a course. This exploratory phase can be the most challenging for faculty. Professors like questions, and frequently generate too many; narrowing the focus to a workable topic is a key first step.

One strategy I have found useful is to apply the five elements of Shulman's scheme and examine questions that emerge as I reflect on next steps for the course. These questions are metacognitions about the course—impressions from practice that may or may not be accurate. Deciding which question to pursue in greater depth may be guided by personal interests, comments from other faculty, discussions with students, consultation of the research literature, or some combination.

Recently I had the opportunity, through a Learn and Serve grant, to revise my Introduction to Psychology course to reflect a stronger emphasis on civic responsibility. I had not taught Introduction to Psychology for ten years and had to update my knowledge as well as figure out effective ways to integrate concepts of civic engagement. The following sections discuss the redesign of this course as a test case for the strategy above, suggesting questions about the newly configured course in the context of the elements of scholarship to help guide a SoTL project.

Vision

A course in introductory psychology is a brief overview of a wide range of topics. The amount of detail presented in introductory textbooks is overwhelming; a critical issue is deciding how to structure the information so students can gain a deeper understanding of key ideas in the field. My course description summarized the inclusion of civic responsibility this way:

> This Introduction to Psychology course is part of a grant collaboration with the Lowell National Historic Park entitled The Lowell Civic Collaborative. The grant will explore civic responsibility, or the "active participation in the public life of a community in an informed, committed, and constructive manner with a focus on the common good" (Gottlieb & Robinson, 2002, p. 16). How do psychologists contribute to the common good? In what ways will studying the science of human behavior help you to contribute more actively to your community?

Questions: Am I adding more confusion to an already overwhelming course? What will I be giving up in content coverage by adding this new dimension? In what ways will adding a civic component influence learning of key course concepts?

Design

The tension between covering material and developing deep understanding is constant in survey courses. In an attempt to address this issue, I used a framework from the American Psychological Association in the multidisciplinary Decade of Behavior initiative (www.decadeofbehavior.org) as a way to place discrete chapters into a more unified whole.

The Decade of Behavior website describes the initiative this way:

> The Decade of Behavior (2000–2010) is a multidisciplinary initiative to focus the talents, energy, and creativity of the behavioral and social sciences on meeting many of society's most significant challenges. These include improving education and health care; enhancing safety in homes and communities; actively addressing the needs of an aging population; and helping to curb drug abuse, crime, high-risk behaviors, poverty, racism, and cynicism towards government. The beginning of the twenty-first century is the ideal time to highlight how insight into behavior will help meet these national challenges, and behavioral and social scientists are encouraged to bring their research results forward to help inform the public and the public policy process about the Decade's five major themes:
>
> • Improving health
>
> • Increasing safety
>
> • Improving education
>
> • Increasing prosperity
>
> • Promoting democracy

Students in the Introduction to Psychology course applied these themes in assignments and projects throughout the course to gain a better understanding of how psychology can help address basic societal needs.

Questions: One of the factors in SoTL involves identifying important questions in the discipline. These questions from the Decade of Behavior are focused on use of research results to inform public policy. Does it make sense to use them in a classroom? Am I trying to create connections that are not appropriate?

Interactions

When service-learning is an option in a course, it can be challenging to find equitable alternative assignments for other students and to organize the classroom setting so that all groups can benefit from the various projects. For this course's individual project, students could select either a service-learning placement in the community (22 hours) with four reflection assignments or two written assignments that addressed the themes through website exploration and connection to the local community.

In the final written assignment, my aim was to create links between students engaged in the community (about half of the class) and students doing written assignments (see Appendix 5A for an example). I also attempted to ensure exchange of student learning through multiple short group projects throughout the semester.

Questions: Was the theme approach the best one to take here? Students working in the community did a good job of noting stories of individuals but struggled to connect to themes. Students doing written assignments had the same problem. Balancing the needs of students in a community college classroom is difficult; it is frustrating when other demands mean that students are absent for small-group projects. At times students seem so overextended in their own lives that asking them to try to connect ideas from others in the class seems unrealistic. Yet how else can we encourage them to begin to consider the bigger picture? Should I try this approach again or move to something else?

Outcomes

My main question here involved how effectively students connected to the theme of civic engagement in the course. Did they "get" the idea that concepts in psychology could be connected to a broader context? In what ways did they demonstrate their understanding? To investigate the answer, I examined many samples of student responses from various projects. (Appendix 5B offers a sample of one exam response focusing on the Decade of Behavior themes.)

Questions: Student responses were not what I hoped they would be; how much is due to the fact that I have not taught the course for some time and was unrealistic in my expectations? What should I do to redesign the questions so they will elicit stronger student responses? Is the main problem the fact that students did not spend enough time reading the text and responding to problems?

Analysis

The use of themes from the Decade of Behavior seemed to be a reasonable approach to broaden the context of an introductory course, but it did add another layer of information for students to consider. Many seemed overwhelmed with the details of the course and unable to appreciate the broader implications of the ideas presented. A major concern for me was how I could get students to grasp these broader ideas on day one.

In reflecting on the various activities I used for the course, one of the group projects showed promise for further expansion. For the project, students were asked to reflect on and respond to a provided quote:

> In a recent article, Lynne Twist (2004) states: "Taxes are not only an obligation; they are part of our role as citizens—not just consumers—in the life of a nation, a political system, and a culture of our making." List the things about this country that you're proud of and happy to sponsor. Why are these important to you?

The students' responses ranged from protecting the environment to funding more soldiers to supporting political parties that would keep us out of war. It was clear that students had passion for the topics they selected; using these passions may help in focusing the material of the course.

Questions: Would it be useful to introduce this project on the first day of class to foster a stronger commitment in students? How could I then weave in civic learning more effectively throughout the semester? What kinds of measures would provide the best evidence of student learning? Developing a systematic inquiry to answer these questions could be the beginning of a SoTL project.

Assessing the Scholarship of Engagement

As noted earlier, service-learning and the scholarship of teaching and learning both aim to create a more permeable classroom where ideas about the course and student learning move out of the classroom, connect to the community and to broader concepts, and then move back into the classroom in a revised form. This permeability creates more opportunities for faculty and students, but it also provides more challenges for assessment.

Assessment Standards

Driscoll and Lynton (1999) contribute excellent examples of how to document professional service and outreach or the scholarship of application; ideas from their volume can be adapted to individual courses in a variety of ways. Similarly, Glassick, Huber, and Maeroff (1997) devised a common language for discussing standards for scholarly work. Practitioners of the scholarship of discovery, integration, and application are accustomed to using such standards as they assess their work.

Applying these standards to assess work in a classroom is less common, yet such standards provide a practical outline for faculty to use in considering their own course revisions or in reviewing the work of peers in a more organized way. They can help faculty place the local experiences they observe in one setting into a larger framework. Faculty can then begin to consider what else they might need to do to enhance the value of their work in the broader academic community. Following are standards and related questions to consider in assessing SoTL, drawn from Glassick, Huber, and Maeroff (1997, p. 36).

Clear Goals. Does the scholar state the basic purposes of the work clearly? Does the scholar define objectives that are realistic and achievable? Does the scholar identify important questions in the field?

Adequate Preparation. Does the scholar show an understanding of existing scholarship in the field? Does the scholar bring the necessary skills to his or her work? Does the scholar bring together the resources necessary to move the project forward?

Appropriate Methods. Does the scholar use methods appropriate to the goals? Does the scholar effectively apply the methods selected? Does the scholar modify procedures in response to changing circumstances?

Significant Results. Does the scholar achieve the stated goals? Does the scholar's work add consequentially to the field? Does the scholar's work open up additional areas for further explorations?

Effective Presentation. Does the scholar use a suitable style and effective organization to present his or her work? Does the scholar use appropriate forums for communicating work to its intended audiences? Does the scholar present his or her message with clarity and integrity?

Reflective Critique. Does the scholar critically evaluate his or her own work? Does the scholar bring an appropriate breadth of evidence to his or her critique? Does the scholar use evaluation to improve the quality of future work?

Applying Scholarship Standards to Service-Learning

Faculty engaged in service-learning often make changes in their courses as a result of feedback from students or the community, but they may not consider how revisions connect to questions in their field or to other existing scholarship. Expanding a classroom project through considering important questions and other scholarship can help it to meet the SoLT criterion of being "accessible for exchange and use by other members of one's scholarly community" (Shulman, 1998).

Can a professor who is revising a class to incorporate service-learning develop a SoTL project to provide evidence of increased civic learning? A systematic inquiry into the question may give practical ideas for translating civic learning into more concrete classroom examples and help to demonstrate the civic promise of service-learning (Saltmarsh, 2005). Showing how a classroom project connects to critical issues in the field and to existing scholarship may demonstrate ways that results can make an important contribution to the field.

Stephen Brookfield (1995) identifies four critically reflective lenses necessary for faculty attempting to improve teaching practice. The first is our autobiographies as teachers and learners. We need to recognize how our own experiences shape our practice. For faculty engaged in service-learning, the importance of experiential learning would likely be a recurring theme across autobiographies. The second lens is seeing our practice through our students' eyes. Work in SoTL and student projects in the community can help to illuminate this more clearly. The third lens, using comments from colleagues, is basic to peer review and the public sharing function of the SoTL approach. The fourth lens, using theoretical literature to understand practice, is also a key factor in preparing to define a SoTL problem.

Faculty who teach at community colleges and engage in service-learning are probably most comfortable in using the lenses of autobiography, students' views, and colleague commentary. Including theoretical literature is valued but often the most difficult to accomplish given extensive teaching loads. In an article on community colleges and the scholarship of teaching and learning, Charmian Sperling (2003) suggests that "teaching wisdom in community colleges is often passed along, like folklore, from one faculty member to another" (p. 596). She goes on to note that the scholarship of teaching and learning "does hold out a promise of something richer and deeper; an element that provides greater grounding, allowing faculty to connect the dots between theory and practice, between one individual teaching strategy and the next" (p. 596).

The scholarship of teaching and learning and service-learning can help to address issues presented in Peter Smith's *The Quiet Crisis: How Education is Failing America* (2004). Smith maintains that we need to adopt a new mindset and rethink what constitutes an education and how we organize and support it. He recommends that we revise our views based on seven core values regarding teaching and learning (pp. 53–54):

- Life is the source and repository of learning. A printed syllabus is not. There must be a connection between the learner's experience and the material being learned.

- The community harbors vast learning resources and opportunities. We learn best in communities, not outside of them.

- Most learners can be successful, and the learner's success is our responsibility.

- College is a bridge to opportunity, not a device to weed out people.

- Diversity is an educational asset to be mined, not a problem to be masked.

- Quality is defined by outcomes in the life of the learner.

- Great teaching is greatly needed.

The first two values clearly align well with the pedagogy of service-learning; the next three values reflect the mission of work at a community college; and the last two values fit with the goals of the scholarship of teaching and learning. Community college faculty who use service-learning and engage in SoTL can be in the forefront of helping to translate Smith's values into daily classroom practice so that perhaps a second edition of his book in the future can have the subtitle "How Education Is Succeeding in America."

References

Battistoni, R.M., Gelmon, S.B., Saltmarsh, J., Wergin, J., & Zlotkowski, E. (2003). *The engaged department toolkit.* Providence, RI: Campus Compact.

Boyer, E.L. (1990). *Scholarship reconsidered: Priorities of the professoriate.* San Francisco: Jossey-Bass.

Bringle, R.J., & Hatcher, J.A. (1995). A service-learning curriculum for faculty. *Michigan Journal of Community Service Learning, 2,* 112–122.

Brookfield, S.D. (1995). *Becoming a critically reflective teacher.* San Francisco: Jossey-Bass.

Driscoll, A., & Lynton, E.A. (1999). *Making outreach visible: A guide to documenting professional service and outreach.* Washington, DC: AAHE.

Duffy, D.K. (2000). Resilient students, resilient communities. In Hutchings, P. (Ed.), *Opening lines: Approaches to the scholarship of teaching and learning* (pp. 23–30). Stanford, CA: Carnegie Foundation for the Advancement of Teaching.

Duffy, D.K. (2004). Service-learning, resilience, and community: The challenges of authentic assessment. In Dunn, D.S., Mehrotra, C.M., & Halonen, J.S. (Eds.), *Measuring up: Educational assessment challenges and practices for psychology* (pp. 243–256). Washington, DC: American Psychological Association.

Glassick, C.E., Huber, M.T., & Maeroff, G.I. (1997). *Scholarship assessed: Evaluation of the professoriate.* San Francisco: Jossey-Bass.

Gottlieb, K., & Robinson, G. (Eds.). (2002). *A practical guide for integrating civic responsibility into the curriculum.* Washington, DC: Community College Press.

Huba, M.E., & Freed, J.E. (2000). *Learner-centered assessment on college campuses: Shifting the focus from teaching to learning.* Needham Heights, MA: Allyn & Bacon.

Hutchings, P., & Shulman, L.S. (1999). The scholarship of teaching: New elaborations, new developments. *Change, 31*(5), 11–15.

Kozma, R.B. (1985). A grounded theory of instructional innovation in higher education. *The Journal of Higher Education, 56* (3), 300–319.

Saltmarsh, J. (2005). The civic promise of service-learning. *Liberal Education 9*(2), 50–56.

Sandy, L.R. (1998). The permeable classroom. *Journal on Excellence in College Teaching, 9*(3), 47–60.

Shulman, L.S. (1998). Course anatomy: The dissection and analysis of knowledge through teaching. In Hutchings, P. (Ed.), *The course portfolio: How faculty can examine their teaching to advance practice and improve student learning* (pp. 5–12). Washington, DC: AAHE.

Shulman, L.S. (2000). Inventing the future. In Hutchings, P. (Ed.), *Opening lines: Approaches to the scholarship of teaching and learning* (pp. 95–105). Stanford, CA: Carnegie Foundation for the Advancement of Teaching.

Smith, P. (2004). *The quiet crisis: How higher education is failing America.* Bolton, MA: Anker Publishing.

Sperling, C. (2003). How community colleges understand the scholarship of teaching and learning. *Community College Journal of Research and Practice, 27,* 593–601.

Twist, L. (2004, March/April). A life of abundance. *Spirituality & Health,* 29–75.

Appendix 5A

Written Assignment: Psychology and Our Local Community

Our local community has organizations that aim to address the themes presented in the Decade of Behavior. Examples include:

- Community Family (health): Dealing with Alzheimer's disease

- Boys and Girls Club (safety): Providing a place for safe activities after school

- Washington School (education): Helping children learn effectively

- St. Julie Asian Center (prosperity): Creating a haven for immigrants to learn English and become citizens

- Lowell National Historic Park (democracy): Establishing an opportunity for citizens to learn about their heritage and role in society

- The Lowell Civic Collaborative at Middlesex Community College (democracy): Offering forums to discuss critical issues in the community

Your assignment is to become an expert on the work taking place at ONE of these locations. You can do this by reviewing material on a website, interviewing classmates who are working at the site, visiting the site yourself, and reading material available. If possible, include brochures or photos with your paper. Select your site and answer the following who, what, where, when, and why questions:

1. Who: Who are the people served at your site? Describe numbers who attend and how the population has varied over time.

2. What: What is the goal and purpose of the site? Are goals being met? Use specific examples to support your answer.

3. Where: Show the location on a map of Lowell. Can it be reached by public transportation? How do most people get there?

4. When: What are the hours of operation? Can members of the community use it at other times?

5. Why: This is the most important question.

    - Go back to the table of contents of your textbook and review the topics presented in each chapter. Select at least four specific concepts from psychology and show how they can connect to your site. Think about this and provide more than a superficial response. For example, a school obviously connects to the chapter on learning, but how does it create an environment for learning? What is the school's educational philosophy?

    - Your site is dealing with improving health, increasing safety, improving education, increasing prosperity, or promoting democracy in our society. As you have learned about your setting, what are some things you think could improve it? As a member of the Lowell community, describe one concrete action you could take to help create this improvement.

Appendix 5B

Sample Exam Question and Student Response

Question

In the last five chapters we have discussed personality, health, stress and coping, psychological disorders, and social behavior. In each of these chapters we reviewed how psychologists have used information to contribute to the common good in areas such as improving health, increasing safety, improving education, increasing prosperity, and promoting democracy.

Think about the various topics we have reviewed and how they fit with the areas listed above. Then do the following:

a. Select one topic and explain it in detail.

b. Then show in concrete ways how it can help in improving health, increasing safety, improving education, increasing prosperity, and/or promoting democracy.

c. Describe one way that learning about this topic has influenced your thinking, perception, or actions.

Student Response

a. Insanity is a legal term; it does not have a psychological meaning. Insanity is the inability to manage one's affairs or be aware of the consequences of one's actions.

b. People who have been diagnosed to be insane are not legally responsible for their actions. It would not be just for people to be held accountable for something they have no control over, such as being insane. If they have the ability to hurt themselves or others, they can be involuntarily committed to a mental hospital. That is why I believe that the legal term insane promotes democracy in our justice system. The innocent (insane) will not be punished for a crime they did not mean to commit, because they do not know what they are doing.

c. I used to think that insanity was a psychological term but not anymore. Now that I learned that insanity is a legal term, I will start to apply the word insane differently. I will only use it as a legal term. I now see that all people do not have control over what they do, and I appreciate the fact that our judicial system acknowledges that.

The Next Nexus: Classroom and Community, Community and World

ROBERT FRANCO

THE KNOWLEDGEABLE, SKILLED, AND INNOVATIVE COMMUNITY COLLEGE faculty members who have contributed to this volume address a wide range of topics that are actually different facets of the same theme. As Kay McClenney notes in the Foreword, to achieve improved learning and community outcomes, we must make significant changes at the heart of the community college so that "students cannot escape engagement." The chapters in this book all offer ideas and models for how to make this happen.

Community college faculty who practice service-learning and engage in the scholarship of teaching and learning can integrate a new set of core values into their daily classroom practice; this change will help drive the reforms so urgently needed in an educational system that many view as failing. For community colleges, educational reform needs to be sourced in classroom practices that connect the learner's experience with the curriculum, view the community as a vast learning center, take responsibility for quality student learning, promote diversity as an asset, and emphasize future opportunity.

This type of reform can leverage and be leveraged by intentional institutional strategies to improve the quality of the student experience. One key measure of quality is the Community College Survey of Student Engagement (CCSSE), which assesses five key engagement benchmarks: student-faculty interaction, active and collaborative learning, academic challenge, student effort, and support for learners. In an age of higher education accountability, many community colleges are using the survey as a central tool for assessing institutional effectiveness. Quality service-learning practice, in classrooms and communities, should result in improved CCSSE results.

To explore this connection between service-learning and the CCSSE benchmarks, Kapi'olani's service-learning program developed and pilot-tested a survey with specific CCSSE items for use with the college's service-learning students in the spring of

2007. A total of 35 students returned the pilot survey. On 28 of the 38 selected CCSSE items, service-learning students reported higher levels of engagement than those students who completed the campus-wide CCSSE the prior spring.

Higher levels of engagement were evident on one obvious item, "participated in a community-based project as part of class." They were also seen on less obvious but equally exciting items such as "discussed ideas from your readings or classes with others outside of class (students, family members, coworkers, etc)," "synthesizing and organizing ideas, information, or experiences in new ways," "making judgments about the value or soundness of information, arguments, or methods," and "received prompt feedback (written or oral) from instructors on your performance." Results from this pilot survey suggest the need for more scientifically rigorous use of the CCSSE in the semesters ahead.

Investing Civic Capital

Duffy's assertion in Chapter 5 that reform in community colleges might contribute to a more successful American educational system in the future represents the profound optimism and commitment to success that rests in the minds and souls of our best community college professors. But there is more than optimism and commitment here.

As America's democracy colleges—and as the institutions that stand at the crossroads of secondary and university education—our classrooms represent a nexus of opportunity and peril for a growing number of young people and returning adult learners. Our classrooms and the local communities from which our students come are also at the nexus of local, national, and global cultures, economies, and ecologies that are rich in opportunity and rife with peril. Service-learning is a central "nexus practice" to connect students to the wider community where they can better understand future academic and career opportunities and immediately address the perils of educational disadvantage and underperformance that are among the root causes of social problems such as poverty, crime, and poor health.

These social problems require huge investments in public funding; public schools and colleges are significantly under-funded in this collaborative and competitive global age. Through a commitment to student engagement in quality service-learning, the civic capital of community colleges can be invested in reducing educational disadvantage and improving the performance of students in under-performing schools and communities. If they invest their civic capital today, community colleges will need to invest less in remedial and developmental education tomorrow, and more public funds will be available for educating local students for collaboration and competition in this global age. More public resources—coupled with accountability for success in educating students to become socially responsible and economically productive members of their communities—will enable community colleges to contribute mightily to an educational system that succeeds for all students.

Community college classrooms are situated differently now than they were even a decade ago, and not just because community colleges are growing into new communities. They are also linked to broader locations through numerous distance delivery systems and the worldwide web. The Noel-Levitz (2007) report "Engaging the Social Networking Generation" notes that 43% of high school juniors surveyed had created a profile page specifically for prospective students. In 2006, a Pew Internet and American Life Research Project survey found that 55% of teens with web access have created a personal profile online; 55% have used sites like Facebook or MySpace; and 48% visit social networking sites daily, with 22% visiting several times a day (Joly, 2007). Some campuses have begun to integrate social networking sites into their recruitment and alumni relations strategies, and web-based social networking applications in the learning process are well underway.

Service-learning can also be a social networking strategy that connects our classrooms and institutions to communities located at fixed longitudes and latitudes but impacted by economic, cultural, and ecological processes that are simultaneously local, national, and global. Our classrooms should be places where students come to understand the nexus of processes, opportunities, and peril, where they learn and act to direct the processes toward opportunity for all, and where they learn that social networks can be collectively mobilized for the common good.

Service-learning provides this critical connection to community for students living in a world that is increasingly fragmented on the ground at the same time that it is becoming increasingly connected online. Faculty, through the unique academic freedom conveyed upon them, can make the scholarly choice to practice service-learning and the scholarship of teaching and learning in their classrooms as a local-global nexus.

Community college classrooms are also situated differently now because of the widening gaps in our society: the divide between urban and rural, between rich and poor, between generations, and between those with and without educational opportunity. Service-learning has much to contribute to students' engaged learning about these gaps and their role in reducing them. Individual faculty, working collectively with their colleagues and well-matched community partners, can shape courses and programs that provide a real-world context for enhanced student learning and increased opportunities for all members of the community. At the same time, students will be learning the knowledge, skills, and attitudes to work with others for the betterment of the nation and the world.

Service-Learning's Most Important Outcome

In a recent op ed column in *The New York Times*, Thomas L. Friedman, foreign affairs columnist and author of the bestselling book *The World Is Flat*, calls the class of 2007 the "Quiet Americans" and describes them this way:

> There is something quietly impressive about this cohort…. They are young people who are quietly determined not to let this age of terrorism curtail their lives, take away their hopes, or steal the America they are about to inherit…they do a lot of their political venting online…they go off and volunteer for public service or for military service with as much conviction as any generation, if not more.

Friedman quotes Stephen Trachenburg, the departing president of George Washington University, as saying, "I've been a college president for 30 years, and these kids are more optimistic about the future than any I have seen—maybe more than they have reason to be."

Friedman applauds the young Americans who continue to sign up for the military despite the situation in Iraq, and who continue to join Teach for America. He concludes:

> And that can-do-will-do spirit is a good thing, because we will need it to preserve our democracy from those who want to steal the openness and optimism that make democracy work…. We have to hope, though, that the determination that characterizes these Quiet Americans extends into their adulthood, and is shared by those who choose to be doctors, consultants, lawyers, and bankers.

As I look at the photos of Kapi'olani Community College's spring 2007 commencement on the college's website, I see students of all ages and ethnicities celebrating their accomplishments, and I wonder: What have we prepared them to be and to do? Did their classrooms act as a nexus between theory and practice, curriculum and community, opportunity and peril, local and global? What did they learn? Did they learn to be willing to act intelligently for the betterment of their community, their nation, their world?

Quantitative research at Kapi'olani (Renner, 2003) has indicated that service-learning students are more likely to volunteer more hours in the community, more likely to feel committed to being involved in the community, and more likely to respond positively to survey items that indicate a sense of connection. Are these findings evidence of a can-do-will-do spirit? Will this spirit extend into later adulthood?

In June 2007, the college's service-learning staff began the daunting task of reading and scoring capstone essays from the 285 students who completed service-learning in the spring semester. We are using an assessment rubric and protocol that lets us "excavate" student essays for "artifacts" that show evidence of gains in knowledge, skills, and attitudes resulting from service-learning.

Through this process, we are trying to assess the degree to which the college delivers on its mission to promote student opportunities for civic engagement and to be accountable to our community and our state. This will also help us be accountable to our accrediting body, the Accrediting Commission for Community and Junior Colleges, Western Association of Schools and Colleges, which insists that our general education program prepare students for lives as ethically and civically responsible members of their local, national, and global communities. The specific outcomes we are looking for include an understanding of the purpose of service, the ability to link theory and practice, a sense of responsibility to the community, personal growth, and development of critical thinking skills. But will these essays evidence a can-do-will-do spirit? Will this spirit last into later adulthood?

We're hoping that this large sample of essays will demonstrate that our community college students have the same can-do-will-do spirit as those at elite universities like the one represented in the Friedman essay. Further, we recognize that civic engagement collaborations with university partners will increase the probability that this can-do-will-do spirit will be sustained into later adulthood.

Annually, conferences sponsored by organizations such as Campus Compact, the American Association of Community Colleges (AACC), Phi Theta Kappa, and the Community College National Center for Community Engagement highlight dozens of students with this can-do-will-do spirit. Whether these students transfer to universities or move directly into careers, community college practitioners remain optimistic that this spirit will be sustained.

A sustained can-do-will-do spirit, the most important of service-learning outcomes, is best achieved through quality service-learning, the scholarship of teaching and learning, and well-matched community-based projects. Single project experiences, even with the most engaging curriculum and pedagogy, are not enough to produce this most important learning outcome. The next stage in the evolution of service-learning in America's community colleges—and indeed in all of American higher education—is for service-learning to be cultivated by institutional mission, sustained across semesters, programs, and degrees, committed to long-term community betterment, and continually assessed and improved. In this way it will be a major part of higher education's accountability to democracy.

When community colleges move to this next stage, we will have even greater reason to hope that the "Quiet Americans" or "Social Networkers" who begin their higher education journey with us will become can-do-will-do citizens throughout their adulthood. If these values are instilled deeply enough, they will remain with students as they move into careers as "doctors, consultants, lawyers, and bankers" and as nurses, teachers, social workers, scientists, technicians, artists, business and political leaders, or whatever twenty-first century careers await them.

References

Friedman, T.L. (2007, May 27). The quiet Americans. *The New York Times*, 4, 11.

Joly, K. (2007, April). Facebook, MySpace, and Co.: IHEs ponder whether or not to embrace social networking websites. *University Business*, 71–72.

Noel-Levitz, Inc. (2007). *Engaging the social networking generation: How to talk to today's college-bound juniors and seniors.* Iowa City, IA: Noel-Levitz, Inc. Accessed August 21, 2007, at https://www.noellevitz.com/NR/rdonlyres/ 425D56C3-9ACD-4A90-9782-70ED7AC3CF2/0/EExpectationsClassof2007.pdf.

Renner, T. (2003, November). *Converging data: Demonstrating service-learning effectiveness on our campus.* Paper presented at the Third Annual International Service-Learning Research Conference, Salt Lake City.

About the Authors

Marina Baratian is Professor of Psychology at Brevard Community College in Melbourne, Florida.

Donna Killian Duffy is Professor of Psychology at Middlesex Community College in Bedford, Massachusetts.

Robert Franco is Professor of Anthropology and Director of Planning and Grants at Kapi'olani Community College in Honolulu, Hawaii.

Amy Hendricks is Provost of the Cocoa Campus at Brevard Community College in Cocoa, Florida.

Tanya Renner is Professor of Psychology in the Social Sciences Department at Kapi'olani Community College in Honolulu, Hawaii.

The authors wish to thank **Roger Henry,** Director of Service-Learning at Brevard Community College, for his contributions to this book.